Colonial architecture in New England

ARCHITECTURAL TREASURES OF EARLY AMERICA

# COLONIAL ARCHITECTURE IN NEW ENGLAND

ARCHITECTURAL TREASURES OF EARLY AMERICA

# COLONIAL ARCHITECTURE IN NEW ENGLAND

From material originally published as
*The White Pine Series of Architectural Monographs*
edited by
Russell F. Whitehead and Frank Chouteau Brown

Prepared for this series by the staff of
The Early American Society



Robert G. Miner, Editor
Anne Annibali, Design and Production
Jeff Byers, Design and Production
Nancy Dix, Editorial Assistant
Patricia Faust, Editorial Assistant
Carol Robertson, Editorial Assistant

Published by Arno Press Inc.

**Library of Congress Cataloging in Publication Data**

Main entry under title:

Colonial architecture in New England.

(Architectural treasures of early America ; v. 3)
(An Early American Society book)
1. Architecture, Colonial—New England. 2. Architecture—New England. I. Miner, Robert G. II. Early American Society. III. The Monograph series, records of early American architecture. IV. Series.
NA715.C63 720'.974 77-14466

ISBN: 0-405-10066-3 (Arno) ISBN: 0-517-53237-9 (Crown)
Distributed to the book trade by Crown Publishers, Inc.

# CONTENTS

# Connecticut River Valley, Part I

THE Connecticut Valley was first settled by exiles from Massachusetts in 1636. The original settlements in Springfield and other communities in Massachusetts and also in the so-called "river towns" of Connecticut, Hartford, Windsor and Wethersfield, broke up from time to time, and the seceders formed new settlements along the river valley at other points. At the same time the first settled towns were augmented by the arrival of new members from the coast. Within a comparatively short time territory was intermittently occupied between, say, Northampton and Wethersfield, over a distance of one hundred miles or so. Their first dwellings were merely cellars, which, however, speedily gave place to a kind of house which became typical of the so-called first period work. The plan of these houses was little more than two rooms on either side of the chimney, in front of which was the stair leading out of the hall into which the front door opened. The second story was the same as the first, although in some cases the rooms were slightly larger by reason of an overhang. This early plan was altered by the addition of a shed on the rear, making the typical plan of the second period, and this again was altered to make the third period by raising the addition a full two stories, and by the consequent change in roofing to the gambrel.

Thence we have shift to the two end chimneys, altering their positions and occupying such a place with regard to the rooms that the resultant plan resembles two of the earlier plans put side by side, with a hallway running between them. These types overlapped each other in various ways, but eventually gave place as essential types to the Greek influence, which began to be felt, perhaps, around 1800.

The Connecticut Valley work had some few characteristics of its own, due to local material or the importation direct from England of craftsmen working in slightly differing methods. The chimneys, for instance, were largely built of stone, since stone was plentiful and brick, of course, was not. The brick ovens which we find inserted in the chimneys were not, as a rule, contemporary with them. The summer beams ran from chimney to end wall, as in the houses of the Plymouth colony, instead of parallel with the chimney girt, as in the early houses of other communities. The use under the overhang of both drop and bracket is a Connecticut characteristic, as are also the brackets under the gable, though the use of brackets under the verge board is not uncommon elsewhere. Perhaps the most striking characteristic of this Connecticut Valley work in the matter of design is to be found in the entrance treatment of the houses. The doors themselves were double doors, paneled in a manner not elsewhere to be found. One writer refers the paneling to Jacobean precedent. The frames around these also were markedly distinctive. Three types stand out, all of which are broad, of course, by reason of the wide door openings: the frames which have the flat entablatures, those with simple pediments, and those with broken pediment frames, which are perhaps more typical than the others. On the detail of all of these, particularly the latter, much careful workmanship is lavished. It varies from a kind which follows precedent to that which is unique, much of the latter being pure inspiration on the owner's or builder's part. It would seem as if the builders of the earlier houses found much entertainment in exercising their ingenuity upon the detail of their entrances, without, however, departing from their general type.

*Photograph by H. O. Warner*

THE COLTON HOUSE, LONGMEADOW, MASSACHUSETTS.
Detail of Entrance Doorway.

THE WHITMAN HOUSE, FARMINGTON, CONNECTICUT.
Noteworthy as an example of the overhang construction with original drops and stone chimney.

MAN LOVES any material that he has worked upon in proportion to its resistance to his efforts of bending it to his will,—assuming that he has not attempted the impossible or the absurd with reference to the task at hand. This is why the hand-hewn timber of our old houses is better than the two by four sawed stud or the six by eight post. I can very well believe that the first settlers in Connecticut took their timbers for their houses with them, as they are said to have done. They had wrought upon them with their own hands, and had a certain affection for them on this account, and what is equally important, the timbers had an affection for the men who had worked them. The frames of our present houses are a pretty good example of efficiency in the economic and modern sense. Its loads have been carefully appraised and distributed proportionately over the members which it supports, so that the strain and stress on each of these is just precisely what each one will bear, and never more or less. This may be all right, as no doubt it is from the scientific or the economic point of view, but it represents for me a very low order of efficiency.

I look at the ten by twelve corner posts in the summer kitchen of my great-grandfather's old home, and I wonder whether he knew that four by six posts would have done the work of these. Perhaps he did, and perhaps he did not, and perhaps he did not care whether it would have done the work or not; but I feel sure that he would never have had the satisfaction out of our smaller post that he must have experienced from the ten by twelve. My great-grandfather had the reputation in his district of being able to square the butt of a log more perfectly than any one else around, and he left a better stump in his wood lot than his neighbors did. I am sure, therefore, that he applied himself with great care to the corner posts, beams and rafters of his own home, that he had a defensible pride in the result of his handiwork, and that he never could have had this pride in any four by six. The affection which he had for his timbers was returned by them, and is being returned to-day. I get back some of it always when I look at the smoky corner posts, or when I lie on the bed in the unfinished attic and let my eyes wander over the hand-hewn rafters.

Connecticut settlers of 1636 forged their way westward from Massachusetts through uncharted forests. They cut their own paths, except, perhaps, for short distances, where they found an Indian trail making in their direction. Besides their axes they must have carried arms; for, though the Indians were politically friendly, they were hardly to be trusted in every case.

THE WILLIAMS HOUSE, EAST HARTFORD, CONNECTICUT.
Characteristic of Connecticut third period work.

They must have carried, too, some provisions and their camping outfits, for they did not know that they would always have luck in finding food, and they were quite uncertain in what places or at what times they would pitch their tents. It is hardly to be believed, therefore, that they carried timber along with the other things on their backs, or that they added this to the burdens of their horses. It is not incredible, however, that, the Connecticut Valley once reached, they had their timbers brought in the vessels which made the first long voyage around the cape and up the river to the place of their abode. They were engaged primarily in clearing and planting, and, no doubt, their energies were fully occupied with these exertions.

The first houses, as we know, were merely cellars dug in the side of a hill, the walls lined with stone or logs; the roofs simply lean-tos brushed or thatched. These crude shelters gave place to better habitations in comparatively short time. The very early dwellings were likely built of White Pine, and in certain instances of oak, squared and bored and ready to be raised and pinned together.

Fetching timber from Massachusetts could hardly have continued long. It was too much like bringing coals to Newcastle. The timber was abundant, and the craftsmen instinct must have cried aloud to exercise itself.

We are not acquainted with the aspect of the forest which these settlers looked out upon, and we do not know precisely the feelings which the native trees engendered under the conditions which obtained; but some of us are not so young but that we have seen native forests, and the impression these have made upon us (though of a later time and under widely changed conditions) is not perhaps so very different from that made on the earliest inhabitants of Western Massachusetts and Connecticut. I myself remember very well the primeval forests of the Alleghany Mountains in Pennsylvania. I remember when I first rode over them on a tote-team, and later tramped my way, with pack on back, beneath the pine and hemlock. The lowest branches of these trees were far above me. I should hardly dare to guess how far, but I can recollect distinctly that the rhododendrons which flourished in the dusk below them interlaced their lowest branches several times my height above my head, and the blossoms of the topmost branches must have been thirty or more feet in height. The butts of the trees themselves were huge, and the whole effect or feeling (one does not observe the forest) for me was the same that I get from looking at a lofty mountain. I do not wish to try to match my strength against a mountain, and I did not (as I now remember) wish to build myself a cabin of these trees.

This was not the feeling, however, of the men who worked among them. These trees, or the making of them into timber, was their life. They were not depressed but rather tempted and exhilarated by the size and number of them; it was their pride, like my great-grandfather's, to square a butt with axes or to notch one so exactly that the tree would fall precisely where they meant it should. They saw only the tree that could be felled and subdivided, barked and piled on skidways and later take its booming way for miles along the frosty slide to water, whence it could be splashed or floated to the saw-mills. These lumbermen had both strength and genius for this work, and no doubt the earlier settlers had it also. In addition, they had an instinct for building their homes.

THE WAIT HOUSE, SOUTH LYME, MASSACHUSETTS.
Unsymmetrical placing of the windows.

The earliest houses which they built have not come down to us. The Indians, who were friendly for the first years, took the war-path, and the life of the settlers for perhaps a hundred years included a constant warfare for defense among its other duties. As the whites increased in number they were more able to protect themselves. The first settlements were frequently destroyed. Springfield was burned in 1675 and Deerfield met the same fate twice, — smaller places even more frequently. Men,

OLD HOUSE AT FARMINGTON, CONNECTICUT.
Gambrel of the third period with plan of the first period.

HOUSE AT HILLSTEAD, FARMINGTON, CONNECTICUT.
Excellent but rather sophisticated example of type of house which embraces elements of design from several periods, all probably earlier than itself.

HOUSE OF GOVERNOR RICHARD GRISWOLD, BLACKHALL, CONNECTICUT. Built 1800.
An unusual and interesting composition in spite of the regrettable bay.

THE HORATIO HOYT HOUSE, DEERFIELD, MASSACHUSETTS
Excellent example of Connecticut Valley variety of a type of house common to New England.

THE FRARY HOUSE, DEERFIELD, MASSACHUSETTS.
North portion built in 1683. An L variety of the above Hoyt type of house.

women and children were butchered by scores and many were carried into captivity. One writer * has said: "There is hardly a square acre and certainly not a square mile of the Connecticut Valley that has not been tracked by the flying feet of fear, resounded with the groan of the dying, drunk the blood of the dead or served as the scene of toils made doubly toilsome by an apprehension of danger that never slept." In spite of this the towns grew slowly, for the inhabitants—such of them as were left—came back and rebuilt their homes.

THE THOMAS LEE HOUSE, EAST LYME, MASSACHUSETTS.
Original part of house built about 1660.

Most of these houses we find were doubtless built not earlier than 1650, and I myself feel reasonably sure only of work as many as ten years later. This, of course, was modeled from the earliest type of house and has the hand-hewn timbers put together according to the logic and efficiency of this early time. The examples of the first period are to be found mostly in Connecticut, and even here in the southern part of the valley. After these, as we go north, we find examples of the two succeeding periods, and in the northern part of the Connecticut Valley we find examples of the Greek influence. This does not mean that the late work is found, but rather that the earlier work is not found (or at least that I have not found it) in the northern part. Here in the valley, as elsewhere in the country, we find the earlier builders the craftsmen of their own

* Holland, "History of Western Massachusetts."

THE DEMING HOUSE, WETHERSFIELD, CONNECTICUT.
Center doorway with one window on either side.

Frame with flat entablature.

Frame with simple pediment.

TWO OF THE TYPES OF CONNECTICUT VALLEY DOORWAYS.

Literal copies in wood of Georgian stone doorways made before Colonial woodworkers had learned the more graceful and more delicate possibilities of wood as a building material, yet early enough to show still a trace of Gothic feeling in the lower panels.

THE FRARY HOUSE, DEERFIELD, MASSACHUSETTS.
Detail of Side Entrance Doorway.
Excellent in proportion and in well-executed detail.

# Connecticut River Valley, Part II

OUR PURITAN ancestors were evidently an uneasy race. Those who sailed into Massachusetts Bay and settled within the present Metropolitan district of Boston numbered among them a group of individuals that after five years found the population so congested as to start them on that western exodus which continued for more than two centuries.

The first body of these adventurers halted at Hartford in 1635, and the following year a second unit stopped at Springfield; and with the growth of these two centers began the development of what was then—and for many years after—the Wild West.

For a hundred years at least this strip of land from Saybrook at the mouth of the Connecticut River to Northfield, a strip about a dozen miles wide and eighty miles long, developed in an intermittent fashion, and during this period the dwellers in the Connecticut Valley above Hartford, were thrown pretty generally on their own resources. Boston was of course their rallying point and objective of their exports and the source of their imports of such material matter as seemed essential to their growth. As for spiritual matter, they were amply supplied—a self-contained community of one hundred per cent efficiency. But for things material, it was a long and hazardous voyage—as long as the trip today "all the way by water" from St. Louis to New York, and by land for over half a century, their only communication with Boston was a trail suitable only for pack horses.

These conditions had inevitably an influence on the architecture of the region. Until local saw mills were established, buildings, either public or private, were of the simplest sort, and three generations of this simple life could not fail to have its effect on the character of the building of succeeding generations. The valley towns in Connecticut being nearer to the sea and source of supplies, outstripped their neighbors to the north, very rapidly in the late 17th and the early part of the 18th century, and it was not until about twenty-five years before the Revolutionary War that any architecture, in which evidence of wealth and a cultured appreciation of it appeared.

But there did appear early in the 18th century most interesting examples of the endeavors of certain builders to carry out with their limited material, tools and a memory more or less fallible, the architectural ideals as expressed in the more favored parts of New England.

The Samuel Porter house in Hadley is a striking example of this struggle to embody classic recollections under adverse circumstances.

It is of more than passing interest, by the way, that Samuel Porter in 1713, the year in which this house was built, was Moderator of the town of Hadley and chairman of the building committee, and that the committee was given power to build the church with no particular restrictions as to cost. It may be that Samuel thought it was an economical time to build his own house. Perhaps he built it for his son, Samuel, who the year before had brought his bride, a Longmeadow girl, to Hadley, and it may be that her admiration of the door-way with its curiously wrought pediment and sculptured pilaster caps, prevailed on her Longmeadow brother in 1734, to use it there as a model, and (very naturally) in doing so, add to its elaboration.

This is mere conjecture as to the Colton house in Longmeadow, but the dates indicate that the Porter door-way may have served as a model for a half dozen others in Springfield, Longmeadow, Westfield and the neighborhood.

It is also probable that Porter received his inspiration from the Connecticut house of the time, for the settlers of Hadley, which then included Amherst, Granby and South Hadley, were a group of ecclesiastical mugwumps, or, perhaps more strictly speaking,

THE SAMUEL PORTER HOUSE, HADLEY, MASSACHUSETTS

Progressives, who after shaking the very foundations of the Church in Hartford, departed in a body for Hadley, in the year 1659.

It might almost be said that the majority of the Connecticut Valley towns were due to theological differences, for in nine cases out of ten, the petitions to the General Court praying that certain portions of the Connecticut Valley in Massachusetts be given leave to incorporate as towns, rehearse the trials and difficulties of the petitioners in adjusting themselves to supposed grievances in Church government.

The period between the close of the French and Indian and the outbreak of the Revolutionary Wars,

THE SAMUEL PORTER HOUSE,
HADLEY, MASSACHUSETTS
*Detail of Corner Post*

DETAIL OF SIDE DOOR—THE CHARLOTTE PORTER HOUSE, HADLEY, MASSACHUSETTS

THE CHARLOTTE PORTER HOUSE, HADLEY, MASSACHUSETTS

was for western Massachusetts, one of rapid development and material prosperity. Roads had been built connecting the valley with Boston, built chiefly through the exigencies of warfare; troops, their officers and the inevitable supplies that went with it, had to pass through the valley on the way to the seat of war around Lake George and Lake Champlain. More delegates found it possible to go more frequently to the great and General Court in Boston and from this time on, the influence of the eastern part of the state is more evident both in interior detail and external form.

Wealth was slowly accumulated; some of it perhaps in a slightly questionable way.

In December, 1764, the agents of Gov. Wentworth of New Hampshire, the Crown's officer for reserving white pine timber, seized in Hadley 733 logs which were all over the 24″ diameter, prescribed by the Crown. Some of them were 44″ in diameter and the townspeople had thriftily detached them from the log drive for their own use.

Over in Northampton two years before this, of 363 trees over 80 feet in length, which had been reserved by the Crown's agents in the fall, but 37 remained in the spring and no one knew where they had gone. There are records of riots in Hadley, South Hadley and Northampton when these unpopular Crown Agents endeavored to do their duty.

White pine was then as eagerly sought for as it is today and the panelled walls of pre-revolutionary houses, testify to the energetic acquisitiveness of our forefathers. Comparatively little grew in the Connecticut Valley south of the Vermont (or more properly speaking, New Hampshire) line.

The records of Northampton, Hadley and other Valley towns, refer to the importation of white pine from the northerly portion of the valley, from which it would appear that all that was used was not the spoil of the Crown.

Pitch or yellow pine, however, was abundant, and was used to some extent for building, but chiefly for turpentine. One individual in Hampshire County, Joseph Parsons, forwarded between 1696 and 1706, five hundred barrels, an average of about seven tons a year, all of which went by the river, sound and sea. In fact, the turpentine industry threatened so to curtail the supply of "candle wood" used almost universally for general lighting purposes in those early days of the 18th century, that the towns are found laying severe penalties upon unrestricted turpentine "boxing."

We were a sturdy lot in this part of the Common-

THE CHARLOTTE PORTER HOUSE, HADLEY, MASSACHUSETTS

*Entrance Detail*

DETAIL OF
MAIN CORNICE

THE SQUIRE
BOWDOIN
HOUSE, SOUTH
HADLEY FALLS
MASSACHUSET

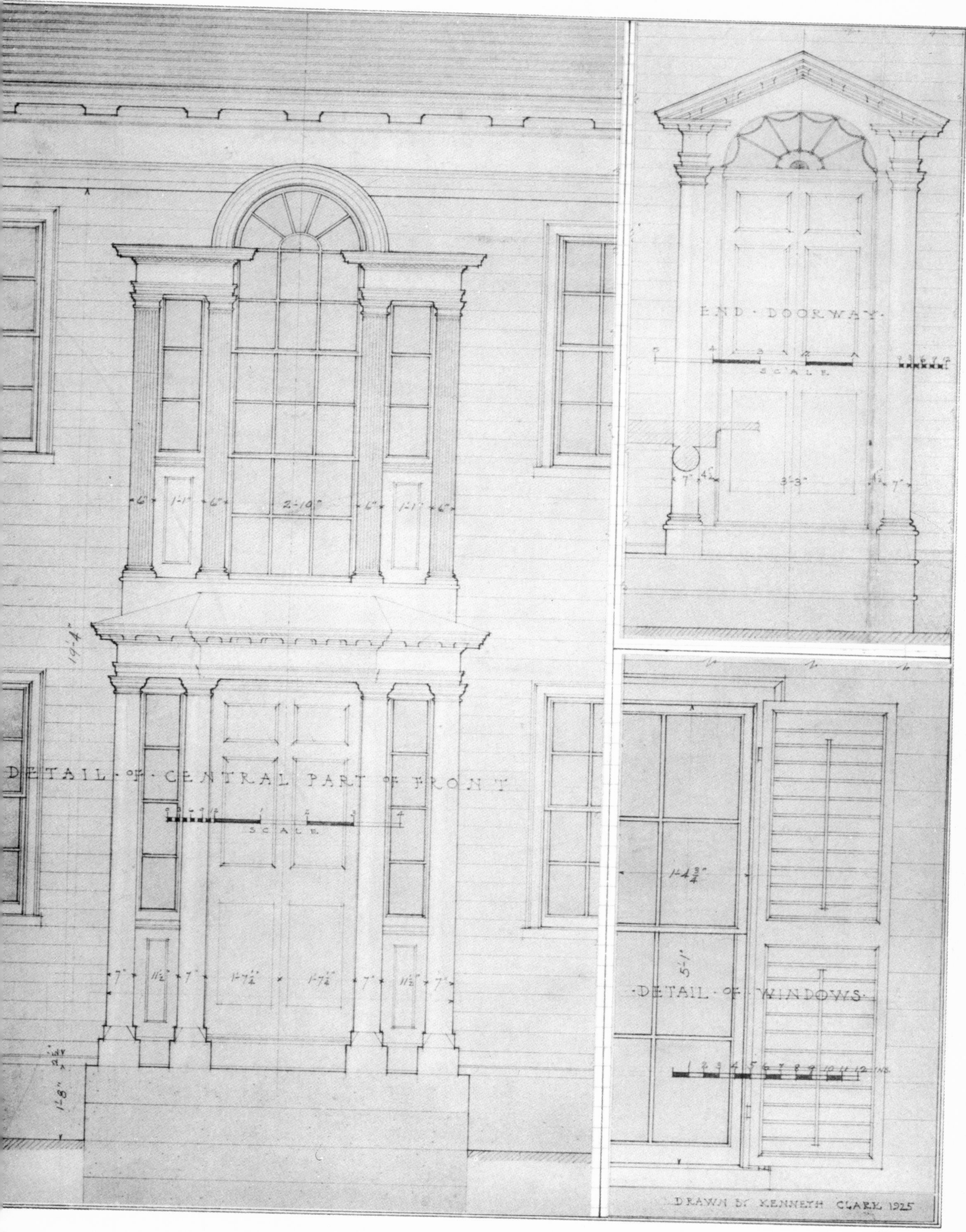

END · DOORWAY ·
SCALE
3'-3"
DETAIL · OF · CENTRAL PART OF FRONT
SCALE
2'-10"
19'-4"
1'-8"
DETAIL · OF · WINDOWS ·
1'-4 3/4"
5'-1"
DRAWN BY KENNETH CLARK 1925

THE OLD MEETING HOUSE,
HADLEY, MASSACHUSETTS

*Dating from 1808*

wealth in those days; the town tax rate in Hadley for example, for the year 1771 showing 369 barrels of cider in the town, which gave an average of four and one-third barrels to a house, none of which was for sale.

From the close of the Revolutionary War to about 1820, the influence of the eastern part of the state made itself felt chiefly in the form of the buildings. The detail was still modified to a considerable degree by the limitations of material and money, and after 1790 was still further affected by the work, first, of Asher Benjamin and about ten years later of Isaac Damon.

Benjamin's first plates on architecture were published in Greenfield in 1797, and the influence of this little book and of the executed work of Benjamin himself, was very great in all the Massachusetts towns of the Connecticut Valley. The Squire Bowdoin house at South Hadley Falls may not have been designed by Benjamin, but evidently if it was not, his "*Country Builder's Assistant*" was in the hands of the builder. The Hadley Church too, as well as the house at the end of the green in Hadley, in decorative detail and still more in form, expresses a strong Benjamin influence.

The various works published by Benjamin after he went to Boston and became impressed with the Neo-Greek revival early in the 19th century, did not so much affect western Massachusetts, for at that period, Northampton had grown in influence to such an extent, as to attract to it from New York, Isaac Damon; and from about 1812 to 1835, he was evidently the leading architect in the western part of the state; his work however being chiefly confined to buildings of a public or ecclesiastical nature.

Perhaps after all, the influence of Massachusetts Bay

HOUSE AT
END OF
GREEN,
HADLEY,
MASSACHUSETTS

on the architecture of the Connecticut Valley is more a psychological than a physiological one.

Generally speaking, the settlers in the valley were less given to the amenities of life than to the stern realities. They lived for several generations pretty well removed from all the luxuries and their time was very completely occupied in labor and border warfare, with the result that a certain austerity, and, one might say, meagerness, tempered their manifestations in architecture, a characteristic which they retained for several generations after the conditions which brought it about had pretty well disappeared. It was rather a striking confirmation of the well accepted fact that the commercial sea-faring community develops more rapidly in an artistic way, than do inland and agricultural communities. But in spite of all this, the persistent endeavor of these fighting farmer theologians to give to their houses and churches, as far as lay within their power, the characteristics that marked the towns from which they came, is always evident.

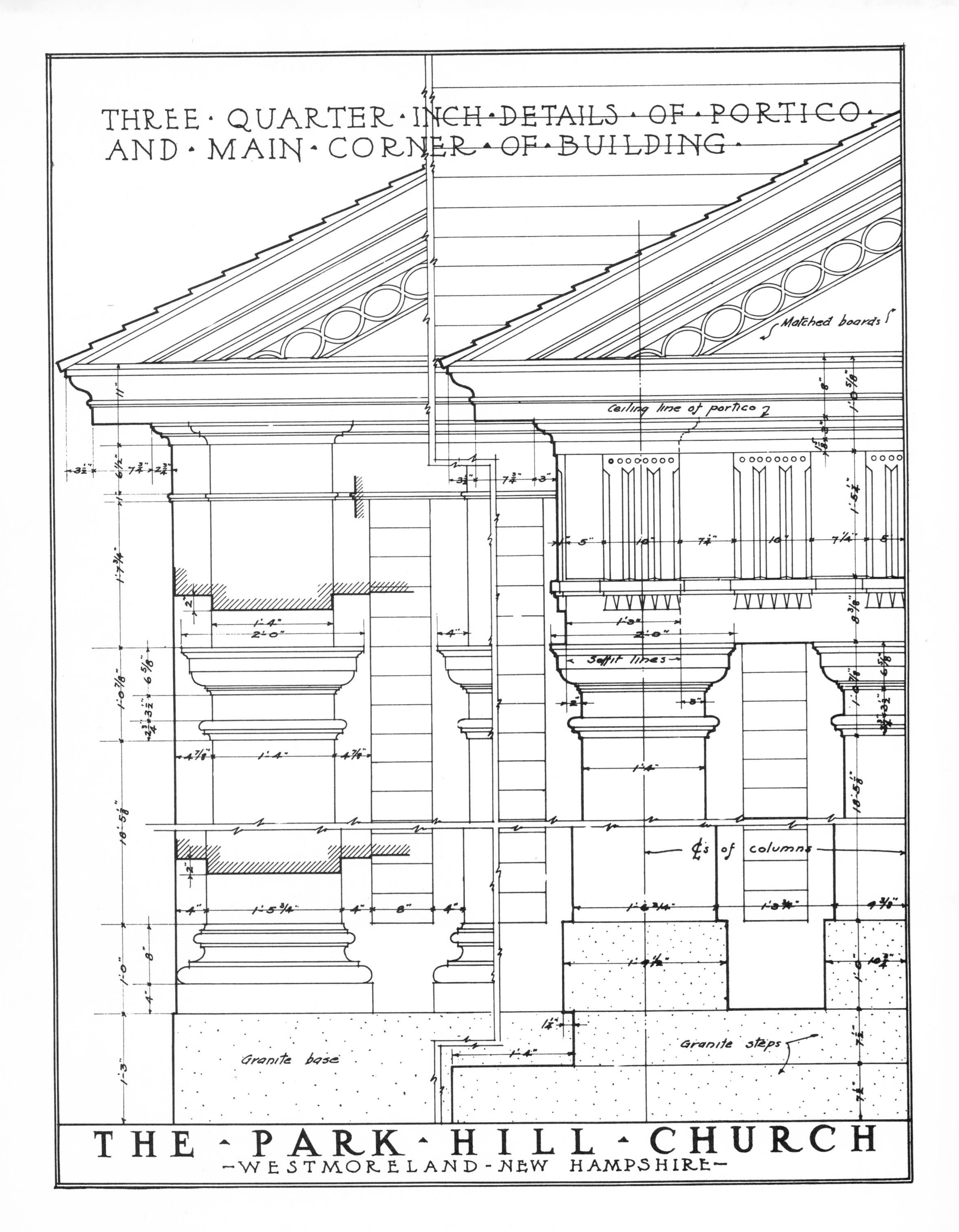
THREE · QUARTER · INCH · DETAILS · OF · PORTICO · AND · MAIN · CORNER · OF · BUILDING ·
Matched boards
Ceiling line of portico
Soffit lines
℄'s of columns
Granite base
Granite steps
THE · PARK · HILL · CHURCH
-WESTMORELAND-NEW HAMPSHIRE-

# New England Meeting Houses

ALONG the middle part of the northern boundary of Massachusetts is a cluster of country meeting houses. They are situated in the south-west corner of New Hampshire and across the line in Massachusetts, in the townships of Ashby, Templeton, Fitzwilliam, Westmoreland, and Acworth Town (near S. Acworth, N. H.)

Built at the beginning of the last century these simple structures are remarkable for the richness and originality of their exterior detail and ornament. They show the wooden country meeting house of a hundred or more years ago at its best.

In many ways they are very similar. They all are set on high ground, fronting on village greens, with their backs to open meadow or woodland and, in two cases, a country graveyard. They can be seen from afar off and dominate, by bulk and height, each composition of town and landscape.

In size they vary from 50 to 58 feet in width, and between 60 and 68 feet in length. This does not include the porch or other motive on the front which in no case projects more than a few feet. At the rear they are square without projections. Each has a bell and an open belfry. Each is surmounted by a tower and an enormous weathervane. The more sophisticated carry the town clock.

Their builders placed them close to the ground with the land sloping away at the rear. Splendid big blocks of granite underpinning support the sills. Big granite slabs with generous treads rise gently in two or three steps to triple entrance doors.

The plans originally must have been much alike. At Templeton the congregation enters directly through a vestibule about 12 feet wide with stairs at each end leading to a gallery above and at each side. There is some evidence that the other churches were originally built in this fashion and that later they were floored over at the gallery level. This makes them now two-story buildings with offices and smaller rooms on the ground floor, though this is not apparent from the outside.

The windows are of the simple double-hung type with twenty-four lights, of the same character as house windows of the period. In proportion the openings are rectangles, in height about twice the width, which varies from 3 feet to 3 feet 6 inches. Three of the churches have eight windows on a side; the two shorter have six and five.

Templeton, built in 1811, is very, very like Fitz-

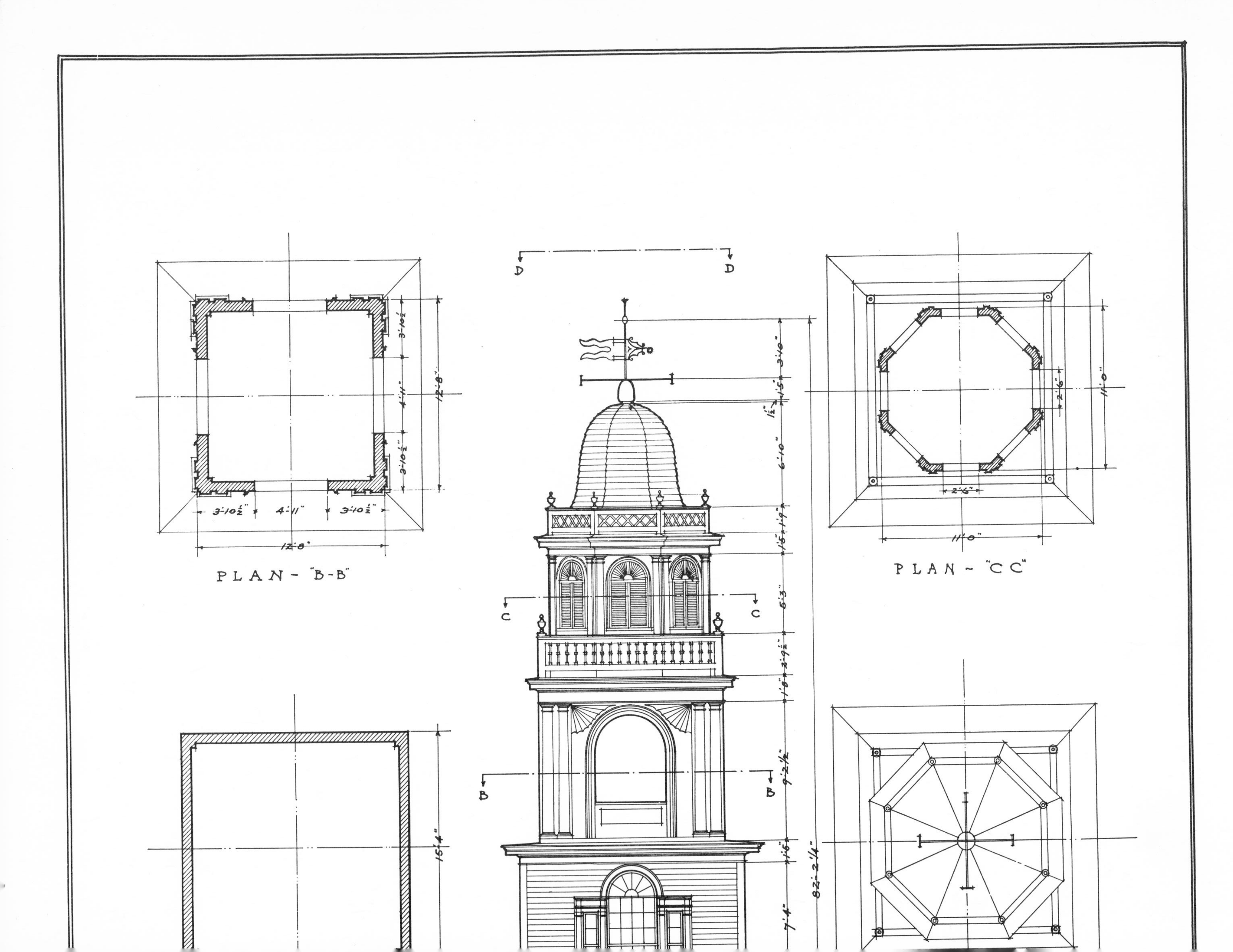
PLAN - "B-B"
PLAN ~ "CC"
12'-8"
3'-10½"
4'-11"
11'-0"
2'-6"
15'-4"
3'-10"
6'-10"
5'-3"
9'-2½"
7'-4"
82'-2¼"
B
C
D

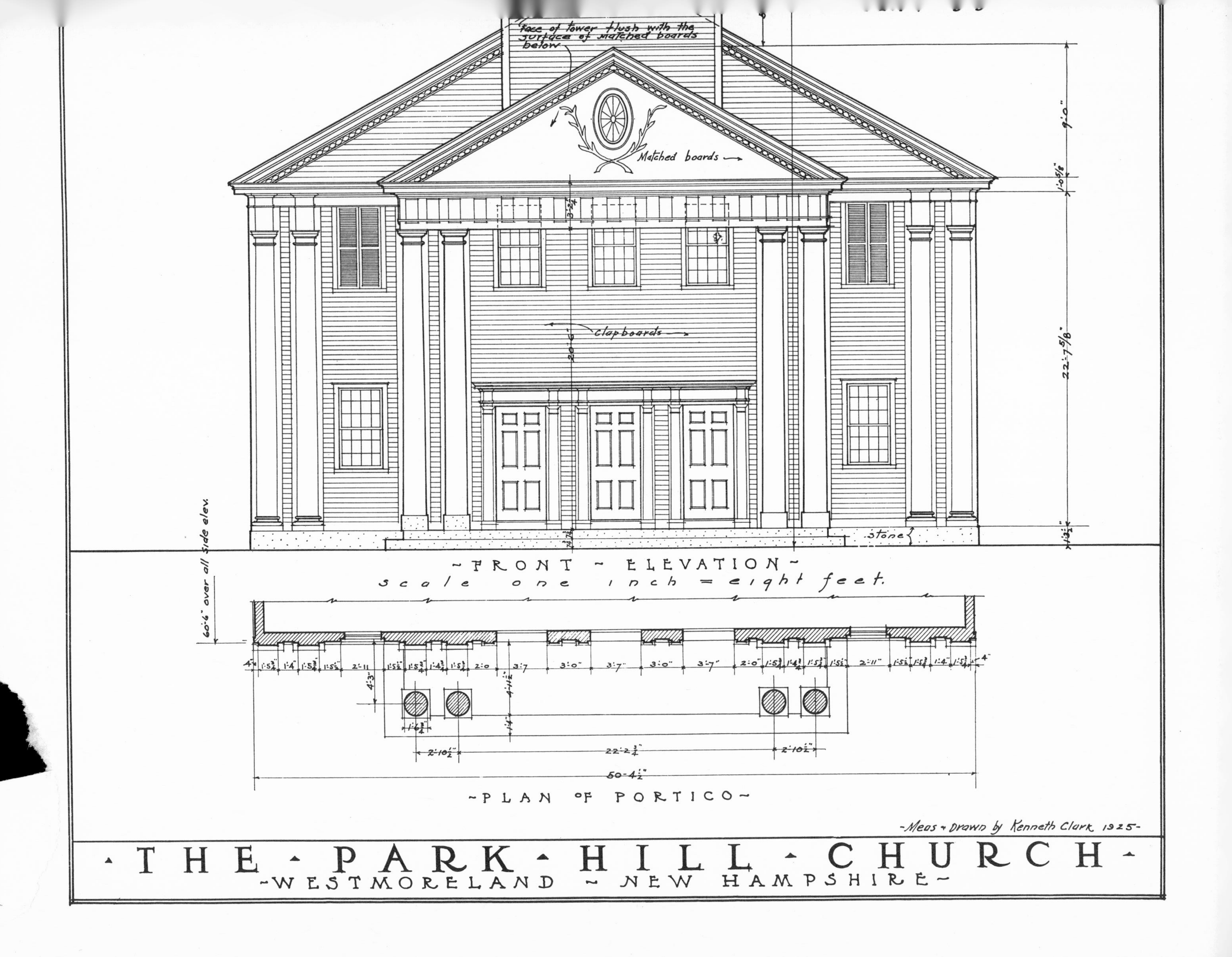
face of tower flush with the surface of matched boards below
Matched boards
clapboards
stone
9'0"
1'0 5/8"
22'7 5/8"
20'6"
3'2 1/4"
60'6" over all side elev.
~FRONT ~ ELEVATION~
scale one inch = eight feet.
~PLAN OF PORTICO~
22'2 3/4"
2'10 1/2"
50'4 1/2"
-Meas + Drawn by Kenneth Clark 1925-
· THE · PARK · HILL · CHURCH ·
~WESTMORELAND ~ NEW HAMPSHIRE~

DETAIL OF PORTICO CORNICE

THE PARK HILL CHURCH
WESTMORELAND,
NEW HAMPSHIRE

*Built in* 1824

# THE PARK HILL CHURCH

## WESTMORELAND, NEW HAMPSHIRE

MEASURED DRAWINGS *from*
*The George F. Lindsay Collection*

DETAIL OF SPIRE

DOORWAY CORNICE

MAIN CORNICE

DOORWAY CORNICE

william. The difference in length is a matter of inches; in width, some three feet. It is obvious that Fitzwilliam, built in 1817, was "taken almost straight" from Templeton.

Acworth Town also, built "about a hundred years ago," let us say in 1825, is almost identical with Fitzwilliam, except that it lacks the columnar porch and the clock and the steepled top. Thus did the fashions move up state. We have been able to compute from these three churches, their dates and distances, that in the early part of the nineteenth century, architectural styles travelled up country at the rate of about 2½ miles per year, a more conservative speed than at present.

In speaking severally of these old meeting houses, we like to refer to them *tout court* by the name of their towns alone. Thus architects are wont to speak reverentially of Chartres or Salisbury when they mean the great cathedrals in those delightful places. This use of "the container for the thing contained" is called Metonymy by the learned. These gave, in the old days, as an example, that short yet pregnant phrase, "He drank the bottle." The meaning, except for the year and vintage, is perfectly clear.

**ASHBY**; Going north from Boston, we come first to Ashby. It is fittingly the earliest, built in 1809, and is a fine simple building, not unlike many other churches in the more immediate neighborhood of Boston. But the beauty of the trim of its triple door, the agreeable scale of its main cornice and the charm of its belfry tower make it one of the most satisfying of its type. The clapboarded Palladian window at the rear bespeaks by its position, the building was originally one-story.

To reach the other churches, we pass over a small watershed and find the brooks now running with us to

CHURCH AT FITZWILLIAM, NEW HAMPSHIRE

DETAIL OF SPIRE
CHURCH AT FITZWILLIAM, NEW HAMPSHIRE

CHURCH AT FITZWILLIAM,
NEW HAMPSHIRE

*Built in* 1817

DETAIL OF ENTABLATURE—CHURCH AT TEMPLETON, MASSACHUSETTS

the westward. From that quarter must have come the new influences to be remarked in their architecture.

**TEMPLETON**, (good summer hotel), is but two years the junior of Ashby. But here we find new variations on the old tune. Hail to the Ionic order, seen through the eyes of a country carpenter, Elias Carter, of Brimfield.

The wide columnar porch, the prototype of Fitzwilliam and Westmoreland, strikes a new though naive note. The intercolumniation follows more closely the proportions of a mantel motive, let us say, than those of classic precedent. The lintel is almost as long as the pediment. We would not have it otherwise. After all the porch is very shallow and the order very handsomely executed. Each of the four columns is carried on a pedestal, man high.

The main cornice is much like Ashby. It runs around the whole church. On the front is added an architrave and frieze. At the corners, Ionic pilasters run to the ground outdistancing the free columns by some six feet. It may be that these free columns once went the whole distance, then rotted at their base, and pedestals were substituted for their lower parts. In the porch pediment we find an elliptical window with palm "supporters."

**FITZWILLIAM**, (excellent old village tavern), is but fifteen miles to the north-east over the state-line. Here we find the same order, cornices, balustrades, windows, doors and underpinning. The tower is almost identical. Painted elliptical "fake" windows at the top have been

DETAIL OF SPIRE
CHURCH AT TEMPLETON,
MASSACHUSETTS

CHURCH AT TEMPLETON, MASSACHUSETTS

*Built in* 1811 *by Elias Carter*

CHURCH AT
ACWORTH TOWN,
NEW HAMPSHIRE

*Built circa* 1825

added and look surprisingly well. A pyramid at each corner of the main tower may well be of later date. The clock is placed somewhat lower, and there is a decorative panel beneath it. There is an engaging scoop in the soffit of the porch to enable a small Palladian window to make connections. The little elliptical window in the pediment has the crossed palm leaves. The building is now used entirely for town purposes.

The misfortunes, perseverance and final triumph of the townspeople in getting themselves a satisfactory church is well told in the Rev. Norton's Town History.

"In September of 1803, Thomas Stratton was paid three dollars and thirty cents for assisting to draft a plan for the meeting house.

"In 1816 a new and commodious meeting house was erected . . . . at an expense of about seven thousand dollars which was a large sum for the people to raise at that time for such a purpose. This church . . . . in every way a noble structure, like churches built about the same time in Athol, Templeton and Petersham."

(Note: Templeton alone exists to-day, in approximately its original form.)

"This church had been occupied for worship nine, or at most, ten Sabbaths, when during a thunder storm on the night of January 17, 1817, it was struck by lightning, fired and totally consumed. . . . . The loss to the people was great, but it served the good purpose of uniting them as they had not been united for many years. . . . . With slight changes in the foundations, the house now standing was erected. This church cost $6000." It was completed and dedicated "one year and twenty days," from the time of the catastrophe.

In this case, according to local traditions, the four big wooden columns were hewn into shape on the spot and hollowed out their entire length to avoid decay. Even then they were placed above the stone porch floor on strange granite blocks with chamfered corners.

**WESTMORELAND**, lies some twenty miles to the north-west. There are a few good old houses about a green, a charmingly placed old parsonage among them, no evident stores or post-office—just a little hamlet, half asleep.

Here we encounter the Tuscan Doric in all its New Hampshire glory. The white woodwork, the dark green blinds, the slate roof and the red cupola make a pleasant picture at the upper end of the sloping common. This church is the smallest, measuring but 50 by 60 feet. While the Ionic orders of Templeton and Fitzwilliam have a diameter of 2 feet, this Doric order is

DETAIL OF SPIRE
CHURCH AT ACWORTH TOWN,
NEW HAMPSHIRE

DOORWAY DETAIL
CHURCH AT ACWORTH TOWN

DETAIL OF PEDIMENT

CHURCH AT ACWORTH TOWN,
NEW HAMPSHIRE

DETAIL OF ENTABLATURE

only 1 foot 6¾ inches. True to form, the shafts rest directly on raised granite blocks. The cornice is much simpler than the others.

The side windows on the top story must have been increased in size when the second floor was put in, all except the end ones at the top of the stairs. "False" blinds, which cover not only these small windows but also a large area of clapboard, are discreetly nailed shut for all time.

We sought information from pleasant people living at the foot of the green who, giving us the key, told us to be sure to climb the tower. This we did and beheld the silvery beauty of the Connecticut Valley. We mounted also the reading desk and there within the big Bible found what we wanted. In a delicate and clear script, "In September 1779 the first meeting was held in our present house of worship after its removal from the now called 'North Cemetery.' It cost to remove and fit up the building 2388 L. 11s. and 6d. . . . . The house remained in this form until 1824 when an addition of 20 feet was put on the front, porches removed (sic) and a steeple added. . . . . . In 1853 it was remodelled into its present form."

This dates Westmoreland for our purpose as 1824. The frame is earlier and the devastating second floor must be the later "remodelling." But the fine belfry and front with their pleasing variations and simplifications were erected only seven years later than Fitzwilliam.

The cheerful manner in which this church was moved about is local legend. Destined for a site still farther from the "North Cemetery," it was held up *en route* by the astute tavern-keepers facing on the green who gave the movers a barrel of rum not to haul it further.

**ACWORTH TOWN**; If one has time it is well worth while stopping in Walpole to recuperate from such extensive globe trotting before motoring up to Acworth Town, a small settlement whose church is "as high as any in the state." It is a cross between Fitzwilliam and Ashby, but has arched triple doors. The tower, though much like its predecessors, is, to our thinking, the best of them all.

In these five meeting houses there is no note of the Greek revival; rather the swan song of the later Colonial classic, sung by obscure rivals of Asher Benjamin. It is written that the late Charles F. McKim on seeing some of these churches expressed an admiration of their architecture.

THE FIRST PARISH CHURCH,
ASHBY, MASSACHUSETTS

*Built in* 1809

THE GENERAL STRONG HOUSE, VERGENNES, VERMONT.

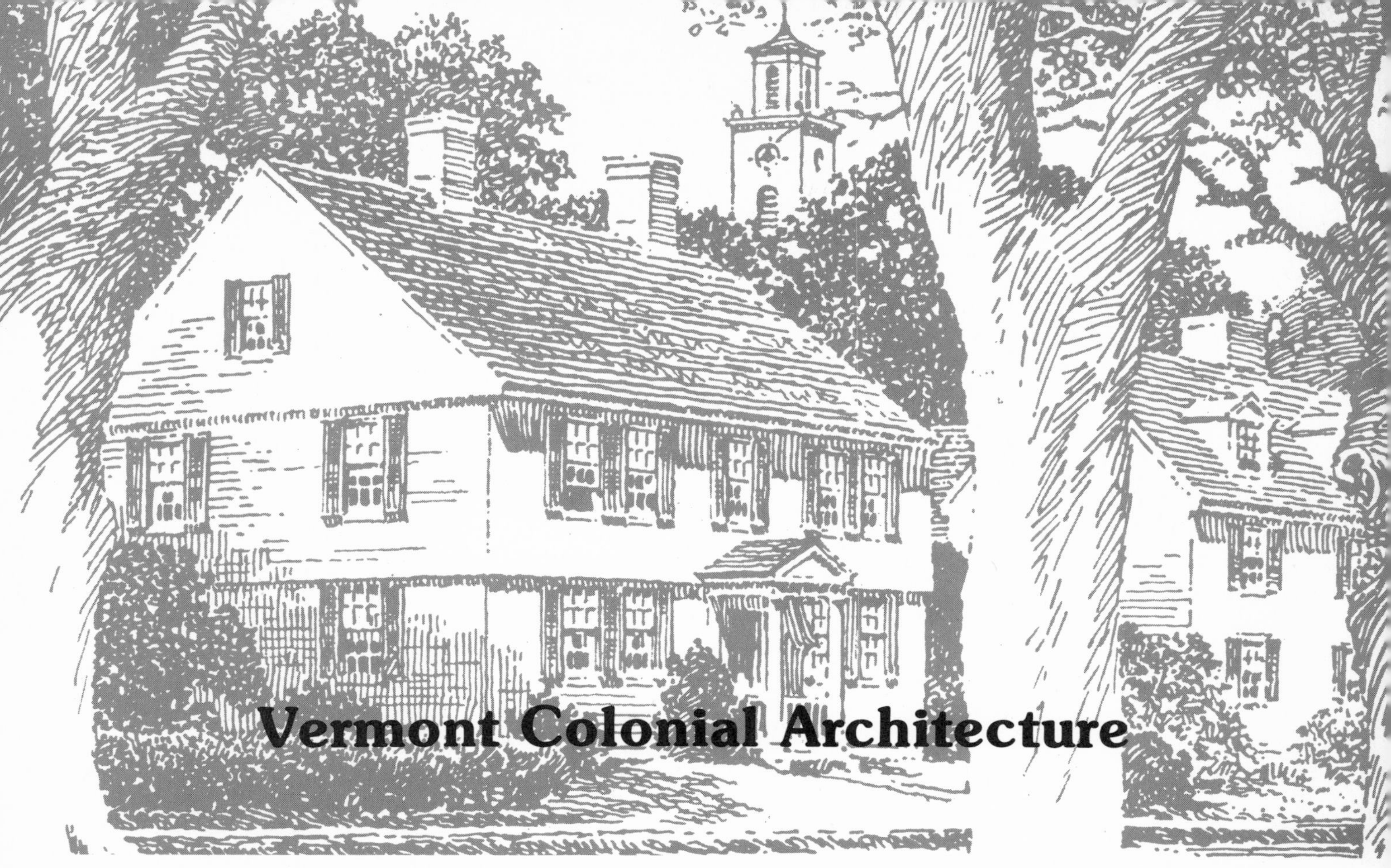

# Vermont Colonial Architecture

CURIOUS and interesting indeed is the invariable accuracy with which the architecture of a particular locality mutely spells its history. Not less engaging is this historic aspect when its lesson lies not on the surface but deeply buried in the meshes of circumstance which must first be explored before arriving at glimmerings of the truth. Such is the case with the fair Green Mountain State. The architectural history of Vermont is yet to be written. It exists, doubtless, not only in the noble houses which have been preserved, but likewise in the town records of many a valley village,—records, praise be, which are gradually being crystallized into useful collections by the beneficent agencies of various societies of portentous and dignified titles, such as the "Society for the Preservation of New England Antiquities." But, as yet, the historians have said little specifically of the charming towns west of Connecticut which, by leaps and bounds, are attaining a national pre-eminence as foci of rest and recreation for thousands of brain-fagged urbanites.

Other sections of what we may properly call our Colonial country have had, each, their scribes. The coast towns, without exception, accessible by main railway lines and the more alluring water routes, have long stood as milestones on the itinerary of the zealous draughtsman, the prying historian and, last but by no means least, the man behind the camera. Who, among the architectural profession or in the splendid brotherhood of kindred souls to whom our old houses are precious, vital things, can look back with aught but keenest pleasure to the occasional visit of that rare character, Frank Cousins, whose valuable records of Salem, Portsmouth, Newburyport and Marblehead were invariably illumined by his quaint anecdotes and observations? The very accent of the man went with the pictures, and his point of view and method of what I can only tactfully term "distribution" were in wonderfully refreshing contrast to the cock-sure briskness of many a brick merchant, refrigerator vendor or miscellaneous patent-pusher who, in normal times, form an unending line at the outer portals of an office.

"Are these pictures for sale, Mr. Cousins?" I asked him, at our first meeting.

His reply was preceded by a look of gentle surprise and reproach which I shall never forget.

"No, Mr. Chappell . . . no,—they are not for sale. I am merely showing them to you. I will leave them here. I know you will enjoy them, and I give them to you. You will note that they are numbered. Keep what you find most interesting,—later, perhaps, if you wish to make me a present, you may mail me a check. What a lovely mantel that is in the Peabody house! I had to bribe Mrs. Peabody with two baskets of Northern Spies before she would let me photograph it," etc.

In Dutch Colonial, Long Island and New York, along the Georgian River James, in Charleston and Savannah,—up and down the coast have ranged the recorders of our historic past,—but of Vermont we find nothing. It is, then, with a peculiar elation that I have undertaken this, with something of the feeling of a humble explorer, a traveller into "green fields and pastures new" in our fragmentary world of architectural letters.

The mass impression, the total result, is perhaps the most trustworthy gauge of value by which to standardize an appreciation. In many cases this is extremely difficult. New England Colonial architecture, in the general sense of the term, runs a wide gamut of expression from the early 17th century survivals—in many ways the most absorbingly interesting of our relics—to the late 18th century period whose delicate life was finally crushed out by the heavy hand of the Greek revival. Each type and phase must be considered and appraised separately, for they are distinct links in the chain.

In Vermont, however, we find a striking homogeneity of architectural expression, an almost unvarying type which makes it possible to judge the value of this little known contribution by a single standard.

This brings me, by a very devious route, I must confess, to the thought expressed in my initial paragraph, namely, that this very homogeneity must perforce have its reason in the actual history of the State. Nor is this reason far to seek or hard to find. We forget, perhaps, that Vermont, more than any of our original colonies, waged for years a most desperate struggle for her political existence. Planted between the great and vague grants of the Colonies of New York and New Hampshire, the green hills and valleys between the Connecticut and the Hudson were a veritable no-man's-land, constantly in dispute, constantly changing hands according to who drew the last map or last had the ear of the King's Council, and, consequently, constantly neglected. While thriving towns were being built in the defined areas of Massachusetts and Connecticut, the wildernesses of the interior were left to the Indians and the animals. It was not until 1724 that the first white settlement in the present State of Vermont was founded at Fort Dummer, south of Brattleboro. The real tide of emigration did not set in until 1760, between which period and the outbreak of the Revolution a bitter controversy was waged between the hardy pioneers who had pushed into the forests, and the more calculating governors of the coastal communities who saw in such exploration only an enlargement of their own boundaries. So acute did this quarrel become that Governor Tryon of New York formally placed a bounty of £150 on the head of no less a person than Ethan Allen, who, later, at Ticonderoga, blazed his way to a glory which

THE OLD CONSTITUTION HOUSE, WINDSOR, VERMONT.

THE WILLIAM M. EVARTS HOUSE, WINDSOR, VERMONT.

HOUSE AT MIDDLEBURY, VERMONT.

HOUSE AT WINDSOR, VERMONT

HOUSE AT MIDDLEBURY, VERMONT

has sufficiently dimmed the luster of his former powerful antagonist.

Throughout the entire Revolutionary War. Vermont fought nobly as an independent, unofficial group of settlers, and it was not until 1791 that she was finally formally admitted into the Union,—a belated recognition which, in the light of her splendid history and services, we should not hesitate nowadays to term "a raw deal."

Be that as it may, here is the plain explanation of Vermont's singleness of style in her early architecture. Of the very earliest, the 17th century and early 18th century type, there is practically none. It was not until the State was recognized and established that its staunch citizens began to build the dignified homes which we find in the lovely villages of Rutland, Windsor, Middlebury, and Vergennes.

The architectural derivation is as clear as the historical reasons for it. One has but to turn the pages of Asher Benjamin's delightful "Country Builders' Assistant, fully explaining the Best Methods for striking Regular and Quirked Mouldings" to see the hand of time pointing with no uncertain finger at the skilful carpenter of Greenfield whose name is writ large over the entire State of Vermont.

The period subsequent to our first stark dwellings, the period of the sturdy Georgian detail of Deerfield and Longmeadow, was still too early for the fluctuating, battledore-and-shuttlecock existence of the struggling colony. Vermont came into full architectural being just after the transition in styles had been effected which parallels interestingly what has happened recently in New York City and, in lesser degree, throughout the entire United States. In a word, the first Adam craze was on,—perhaps not the *very* first, but leaving the great original out of the discussion, the first architectural Adam was certainly the great popular style of the new State. It was between 1773 and 1798 that Robert and James Adam published the splendid series of engravings of their undying monuments to a phase of English architecture which stands for the utmost delicacy and refinement of Britain as clearly as Louis Seize indicates the culture of France. This was the fount from which Asher Benjamin drew his inspiration. His vessel was no royal tankard, but the water it held was pure. Far from being a servile copyist, he translated the proportions of cornice and column from terms of stone to wood with a niceness of judgment and delicacy of appreciation of the material he was working in that has earned him an undying and enviable place in the architectural history of America.

THE WAINWRIGHT HOUSE, MIDDLEBURY, VERMONT.

HOUSE AT WINDSOR, VERMONT.

HOUSE AT MIDDLEBURY, VERMONT.

THE SHERMAN EVARTS HOUSE, WINDSOR, VERMONT.

HOUSE AT CASTLETON, VERMONT.

ENTRANCE DETAIL.
MEECHAM-AINSWORTH HOUSE, CASTLETON, VERMONT.

THE FULLERTON HOUSE, WINDSOR, VERMONT.

THE JOHONNOT HOUSE, WINDSOR, VERMONT.

HOUSE AT CASTLETON, VERMONT.

Strange, how history repeats herself! The hotels, the many new apartment houses on Park Avenue, in New York,—everywhere we are rushing to Adam. It is a fad, a phase, a transitory enthusiasm, but it will leave charming results behind it. If I were asked to coin a modern expression for the early architecture of Vermont, I should say they did "wooden Ritz" —and I think I should be understood.

It is a sophisticated art, but an art still sound and vigorous. Canons of judgment in these matters are peculiarly personal, and my individual rating of our national periods gives first place to the earlier, more naïve structures in which the broader elements of mass and proportion, fenestration and austere profile seem to fall into a harmony that is inevitable and was, probably, unconscious. Vermont is not without her style, as in the old Constitution House in Windsor, built in 1777, and restored with a reverent regard to the ancient law of severity.

THE WAINWRIGHT HOUSE,
MIDDLEBURY, VERMONT.

More characteristic by far, however, are such bits of pure Adam detail as the charming door of the Sherman Evarts House, also in Windsor, or the ingenious interlaced frieze on one of the stately residences of Middlebury, known as the Wainwright House, which strikingly illustrates the addition to a classic background of a motive which could be properly executed in wood, and wood alone.

Less fortunate, but of singular interest in illus-

THE SHERMAN EVARTS HOUSE, WINDSOR, VERMONT.

trating a subtle approach to the decadence of over-refinement, is the curious porch of the Meecham-Ainsworth House in Castleton where we see the ingenuity of the skilful workman combining three types of arches, the semicircle, the elliptical and the stilted, in a single motif. Far more than the usual refinement in design and proportion are found in the General Strong House at Vergennes. Here General Strong lived while he and Macdonough were building the fleet which won the Battle of Lake Champlain.

In general, we may say of the Colonial architecture of Vermont that it was a true and dignified expression of the economic conditions of its period, nor can we ask more of any generation. In its studious development of classic ornament and general excellence of taste it goes far to rebut the quaint assumption of J. Norman, an earlier precursor of Asher Benjamin, who prefaces his hand-book with the encouraging statement that architecture should be universally practiced, as it is "so easy as to be acquired in leisure times, when the Business of the Day is over. . . ."

THE SHERMAN EVARTS HOUSE,
WINDSOR, VERMONT.

I herewith formally pin upon Mr. Norman's breast a medal, proclaiming him to be the great originator of that vast army of home-builders who firmly believe that they planned their own houses and that the architect merely drew some white lines on blue paper putting on some figures and arranged the staircase so that it did not end in the living-room fireplace.

THE GENERAL DAVID ROBINSON HOUSE, OLD BENNINGTON, VERMONT.
A unique adaptation of the Palladian window
used frequently in the vicinity of Bennington.

# Bennington, Vermont

WE are continually reading more or less romantic tales of early Colonial life woven in and about houses with low-ceilinged rooms whose adze-hewn beams, dark with time and cavernous fireplaces, bring forth memories of a past filled with the simplicity of a cheerful hospitality. These descriptions, while adequate and true as to detail in recalling the past, seldom fail to include the time-worn bromide "They knew how to build in those days." So naturally one might be led to believe that here is the reason for the present revival of interest in Colonial architecture. But if this were true we would see at every hand replicas of this wonderful era, having true beamed ceilings and corner posts with braces projecting into the room. This is not the case, however, and it is not because of plumbing, wiring, or the other practical necessities of a modern house, but for the simple fact that the present-day builder asks for the Colonial style because of its exterior beauty rather than for any merits of good old-fashioned construction.

The secret of this desire for the Colonial has been the result of an unconscious appreciation of the color and texture as well as the form of these early houses. The motorist, passing through one of the quiet old villages with its ancient elms shading the beautiful old houses, cannot but retain delightful impressions of their simplicity and charm, and carry away with him a desire to recreate for himself something of that same potent quality which lingers in his mind. The dark roofs with their huge old chimneys, the green shutters, hung against broad white clapboards, shingled or weather-beaten surfaces, as well as the perfect detail of the ornament used on old doorways, cornices, and porches, serve to create an impulse for better building and unconsciously cause a truer appreciation of the relative value of textures, color, and form.

While methods of construction are, to-day, slightly different, due to the change in conditions and in the variety of inventions, still the results may readily be, to all intents, identical. The material is always the same, though the near-by forest is changed to the near-by lumber-yard. The old beams, so readily felled, squared with an adze, and hoisted into place to bear the weight of construction, are substituted to-day by beams of a uniform size, sawed by mechanical means and of an adequate strength for the load they are to bear. And so on through the details of construction, for what we emphasize as accounting for the charm and permanency of old work can be as readily obtained to-day should we so desire. We need not necessarily follow the early methods, if the proper relation of values in the Colonial detail is understood and studied in the design. The early builders did their work in the simplest and most practical way possible to them—if we were to employ their methods we should have no better results than by using modern methods, and would only incur an unnecessary amount of labor and expense.

There are such a variety of details to be understood. Take, for example, the clapboards; their width or exposure to the weather is of vital importance, their edges may be rounded by many coats of paint, or possibly they may have little half round beading at the drip edge. What is their relation to the cornice boards, door and window frames? How do they meet the underside of the cornice and finish at the base? Are they surrounded by a plain or molded surface? What about the width of these clapboards? It is the finesse thus displayed by the early builder that causes us to exclaim as we approach and study his work. It is these things that combine to make his achievement pleasing.

As time went on the early builder developed more studied and elaborate detail; this, added to his already beautiful use of plain surfaces, served to enhance the proportion of his doors, windows, and cornices. The early examples were naturally quaint and rather archaic, with odd curves and shapes, and were only a step removed from the forms of the old world which they were trying to recall and emulate. Documents were gradually assembled and the designs took on a more studied and classical character, recalling in a thoroughly adequate manner the most perfect Georgian and Adam detail. As the early craftsmen designed they had always the actual structure in mind, a light here and a shadow there, the suitability of the detail they adapted, and they were not fooled as many of our modern designers have been by the sparkle achieved by lines crossed at the ends, inevitable axis lines and facile swerves of the pencil on paper. Modern American architecture has often been cursed because of clever draughtsmen who see only the paper in front of them rather than the structure beyond.

THE HINSDALE HOUSE, NORTH BENNINGTON, VERMONT.
Another example of the use of the adapted Palladian window.

There are other weaknesses that our draughtsmen must overcome before we achieve that atmosphere of repose and respectability associated with the old houses. For instance the proneness to indulge in petty conceits, sprinkling them liberally over the design; working all of their pet motifs into the one before them. They should be more conservative and use possibly two in an effective manner, thereby adding visibly to the result and gaining a design of a more restful and pleasing character. Among the

THE HENRY HOUSE, NORTH BENNINGTON, VERMONT Built in 1769.

little conceits referred to are the multitude of flower pot, singing bird, and new moon patterns that are cut in shutters, wrecking completely the exquisite, soft, velvety texture of the molded panel. Then, not infrequently, we see a recurrence of the fad of projecting the rafter ends to the underside of the cornice, and, still more, the exotic cut-outs on latticework, the overdoing of shutter fasts, hanging door lamps, queer ironwork, and patterned brick porches and steps, instead of the old, weathered, stone ones or soft, rich, thin bricks laid without mortar.

Bennington, Vermont, and the neighboring towns were on the edge, the frontier of colonization, while the sea-coast towns were quite the center of it. One does not find in these examples the perfection which might have been achieved if they had been in the center of a greater field of activity and experiment, yet several interesting motifs have been developed in Vermont, not to be found in other localities.

The type of house to be found near Bennington seems to be similar to that built in great numbers in the north Connecticut valley. It is narrow and rectangular in plan. Some are merely box-like structures, but well proportioned with excellent window and door openings.

Before entering into a discussion of the characteristics of the Vermont houses, there is one of a more unusual type which demands attention. This is the Henry house at North Bennington, built in 1769. The porch, with its square columns, gives an atmosphere unique in houses of the north. Its proportions are generous, the roof lines simple, chimneys good, the detail, especially of the columns, slightly crude. Such little touches as the wooden benches and long slanting leader give an added quaintness. The clapboards are wide and the corner boards, as well as the corners of the square columns, have beaded edges. Our modern work often forgets the edges, one of the little refinements which make us enthusiastic and pleased with the old. Analyzing the general scheme we find it a large proportion of gray in the clapboards, a dark space in the shade of the porch relieved by the white of the columns. The doors and windows with the accompanying deep-colored shutters are placed casually.

The Henry house, although of early date, has a more home-like and hospitable atmosphere than some of the later and more typical rectan-

THE HAWKINS HOUSE, SOUTH SHAFTSBURY, VERMONT.

THE HAWKINS HOUSE, SOUTH SHAFTSBURY.

THE KNEELAND HOUSE, HARTFORD.

THE COVERNOR GALUSHA HOUSE, SOUTH SHAFTSBURY, VERMONT.

gular houses of this section. They were box like in shape, ornamented at the doors, windows, and cornice. The carpenter builders became more skilful as they created new structures from year to year, although several houses are very similar.

A detailed triple window has been used over front entrances several times. This form is adapted from the Palladian window and is the unusual feature of some of the houses illustrated in this chapter. Instead of the entablature being placed above the pilasters the central semi-circular architrave rests directly on the caps. The remainder of the cap is taken up by the architrave of the smaller arches. The sills return around the plinth and have small molded brackets supporting the pilasters. Appearing as this motif does three times in the houses illustrated, they must have been built by the same carpenter, or else this feature was one of the earliest stock details. The Colonial builders always had difficulty in placing such details as Palladian windows because they endeavored to build them into the usual plain front, without considering their relation to the windows on each side. They placed the meeting rail in an awkward manner, making unpleasant divisions of glass. This is an important point, since many good designs are spoiled because panes of different sizes are used throughout a house.

THE GENERAL DAVID ROBINSON HOUSE, OLD BENNINGTON, VERMONT.

The Palladian window in the Hinsdale house has been regrettably changed by the removal of the original sash. It is not as much in character with the surrounding detail as is the one in the Governor Galusha house at South Shaftsbury,

HOUSE AT WEATHERSFIELD, VERMONT.

and yet it in turn is not as interesting as the remarkable window in the house of General David Robinson at Old Bennington. Realizing the weakness of this feature in the Governor Galusha house the carpenter builder applied pilasters to the main wall of the Robinson house, thereby separating it from the side windows and linking it with the entrance porch.

Studying these three houses, the Hinsdale house is consistent and good in scale, except for the aforementioned triple window. The rich gray clapboards, strengthened at the corners by the nicely proportioned quoins capped by the sturdy cornice with delicate dentil-like brackets and relieved by the very simple and rich architraves of the window, denote it as the work of a skilful designer. The door detail is quite in harmony.

Of the Governor Galusha house much might be said about the porch; well might we remember this example when designing for a client who demands a wide generous entrance. Unfortunately the main roof has not its generous spread. The cornice is good in itself but it lacks the feeling of support and the window-sash have been changed to panes of a larger glass size. This is unfortunate, for you will find that the most satisfying designs are ones having uniform sizes of glass. The size of glass in the triple window is perfect, and it is regrettable that this size was not used over the entire house. The chimneys are not large enough to be consistent in design with the other details of the house.

The General David Robinson house has the most developed treatment of texture, the strong whites of the porch against the gray of the clapboards, pilasters, and wall, with the exquisitely divided sash softening the dark openings flanked by shutters. The detail throughout is delightful in scale. This house is perhaps one of the most beautiful of the examples in this.

A house with a similar *partis* but weak in the duplication of pediments and stronger than the General Robinson house in the pilaster treatment is the Hawkins house at South Shaftsbury. Here, instead of stopping over the front, they carry around and become definite supporting corners to the design. The play of light and shade is masterly, the soft velvety whites of the pilaster, pediment, and window heads, the background of gray and the well-shaped dark openings make it perhaps the most balanced ex-

THE GALUSHA HOMESTEAD, SOUTH SHAFTSBURY, VERMONT.

ample of texture, but lacking a predominant feature such as exists in the General Robinson house. The double columned entrance is seldom found, though it might have been more satisfying to have projected the columns farther and separated them slightly to give a deep shaded entrance.

The other two groups, with Palladian windows, with and without pilasters but possessing gable-ends, have combined motifs to make the General Robinson house. We then find a third group of rectangular houses with very flat hip roofs, such as the house at Weathersfield, still showing signs of its previous refinement, and the house at Norwich combining characteristics with the Governor Galusha house and the Hawkins house to give us the Leach house at Pawlett.

This may not have been what happened, but was some similar series of events. In the first two Adam details have been used to ornament the frieze over the first-story windows, the Weathersfield house having a door rather common to this type and a boxy cornice with small curved brackets, while the Norwich house repeats the window-frieze design very happily in the frieze of the main cornice. The door of this house is perhaps a bit small in size and too intimate in detail, although in itself a most beautiful bit.

As descendants show a likeness to their forebears with here and there a peculiar outcropping of curious characteristics, so in these homes there are the fortunate few having all the refinement of the examples inspiring their chief characteristics while occasionally one finds odd off shoots not wholly explainable. There is the long and narrow form represented by the Saywood house at Woodstock, Vermont, with a none too exciting door, while the large and cumbersome type includes the Kneeland house at Hartford, Vermont.

THE HAWKINS HOUSE, SOUTH SHAFTSBURY, VERMONT.

THE GENERAL DAVID ROBINSON HOUSE, OLD BENNINGTON, VERMONT.

THE KNEELAND HOUSE, HARTFORD, VERMONT.

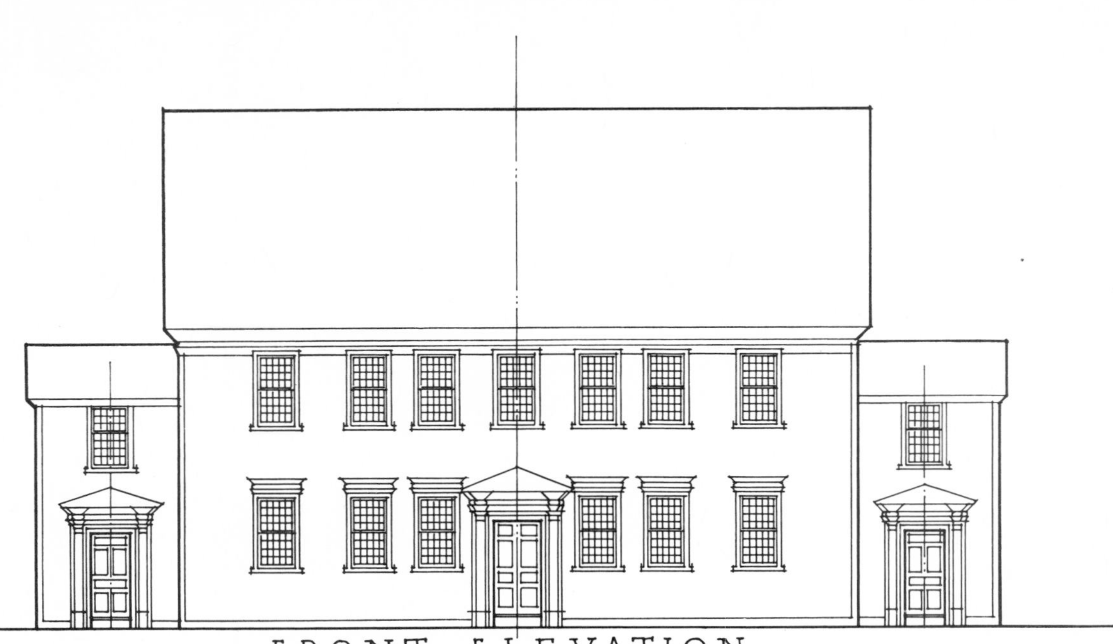

·FRONT·ELEVATION·

BUILDING·WAS·STARTED·IN·1787·AND COMPLETED·ABOUT·1800·THE·STRUCTURE·WAS·USED·AS·A·MEETING·HOUSE·FOR·RELIGEOUS·PURPOSES·UNTIL·ABOUT·1839·WHEN·IT·WAS·CONVERTED·FOR·USE·AS·A·PLACE·FOR·TOWN MEETINGS·AT·THAT·TIME·THE·PULPIT AND·THE·THREE·ROWS·OF·LONG·PEWS·IN·FRONT·OF·IT·WERE·REMOVED: IN·1869·THE·BUILDING·WAS·ABANDONED·AND·REMAINED·UNUSED AND·NEGLECTED·UNTIL·THE·YEAR OF 1907·WHEN·A·FUND·WAS·RAISED FOR·RESTORATION: THE·PULPIT·AND THE·THREE·LONG·PEWS·WERE·REPLACED·BY·REPRODUCTIONS·WHICH·WERE·AS·NEAR·AS·POSSIBLE·TO·THE ORIGINALS·AND·THE·ENTIRE·BUILDING PUT·IN·GOOD·CONDITION·THE·BUILDING IS·OF·WHITE·PINE·THROUGHOUT·WITH·THE·EXCECEPTION·OF·THE·PARTS·OF THE·INTERIOR·WHICH·WERE·RESTORED THESE·ARE·OF·CALIFORNIA·RED·WOOD·USED TO·MATCH·THE·OLD·WHITE·PINE·OF·THE INTERIOR·WHICH·HAD·NEVER·BEEN·PAINTED·OR·FINISHED·IN·ANY·WAY AND·HAD·AGED·TO·A·BEAUTIFUL·GOLDEN·BROWN·

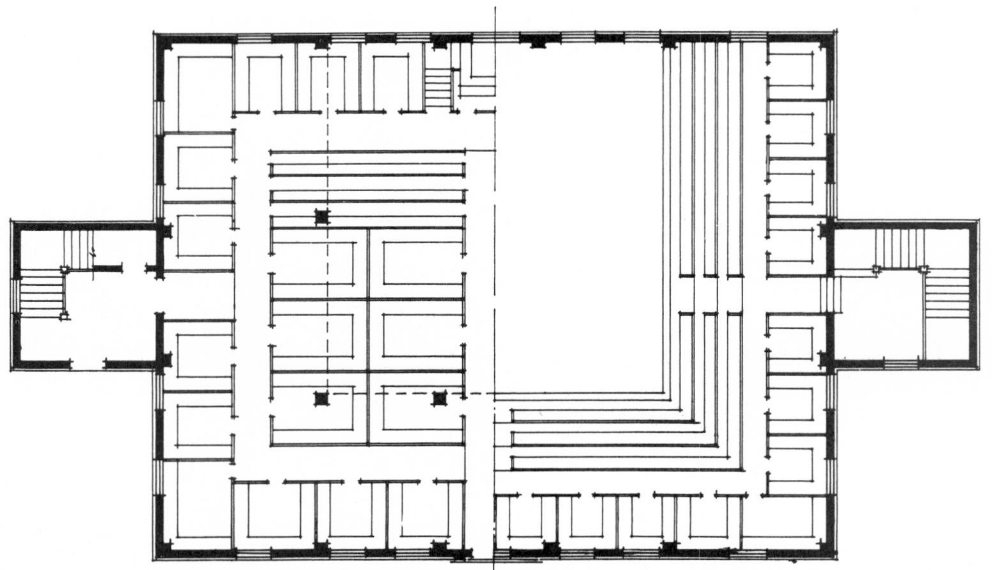

½ FIRST·FLOOR·PLAN | ½ GALLERY·PLAN

SCALE FOR ELEVATION & PLANS 1/16" = 1'-0"

0 2 4 6 8 10 12 14 16 18 20 22 24 26 28 30 32 FEET

Meas & Drawn – Kenneth Clark·1927·

# THE·ROCKINGHAM·MEETING·HOUSE
## ·ROCKINGHAM·VERMONT·

# Rockingham, Vermont Meeting House

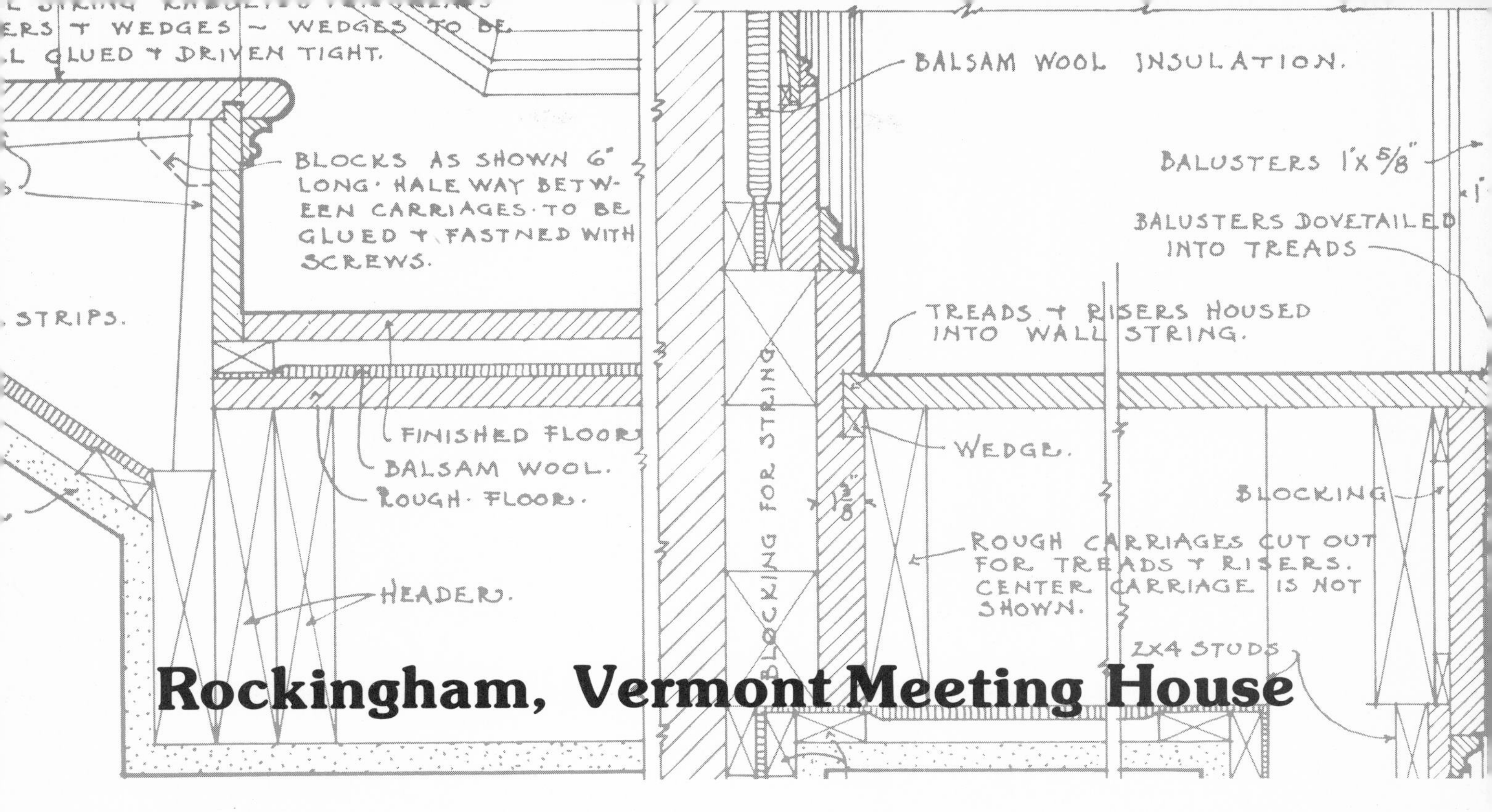

GENERAL VIEW OF FRONT ELEVATION AND ENCLOSED ENTRY

CENTRAL FRONT DOOR – THE ROCKINGHAM MEETING HOUSE, ROCKINGHAM, VT.

*Entablature of Side Door* *Entablature of Front Door*

THE ROCKINGHAM MEETING HOUSE, ROCKINGHAM, VERMONT

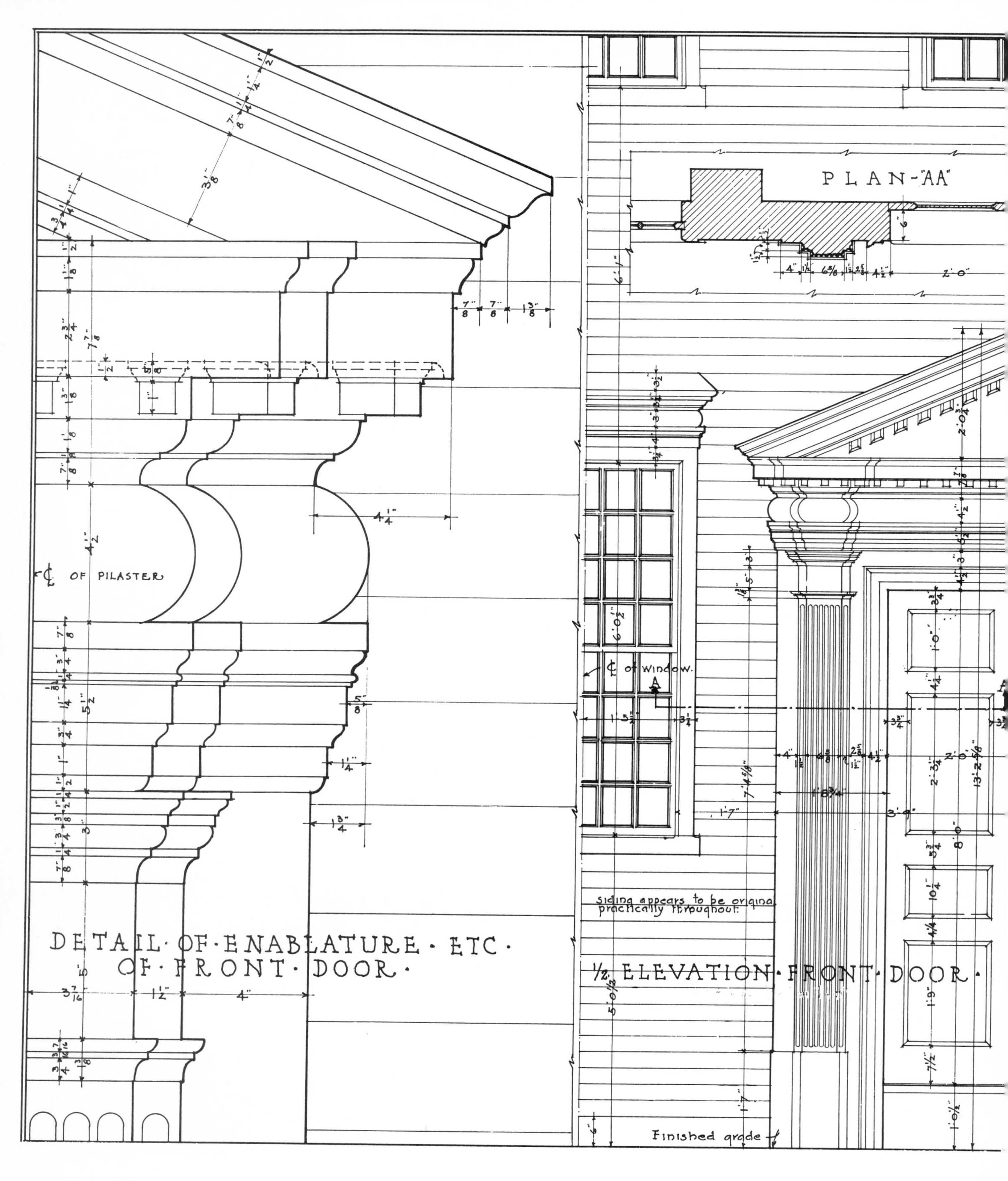


THE · ROCKINGHAM

· ROCKINGHAM

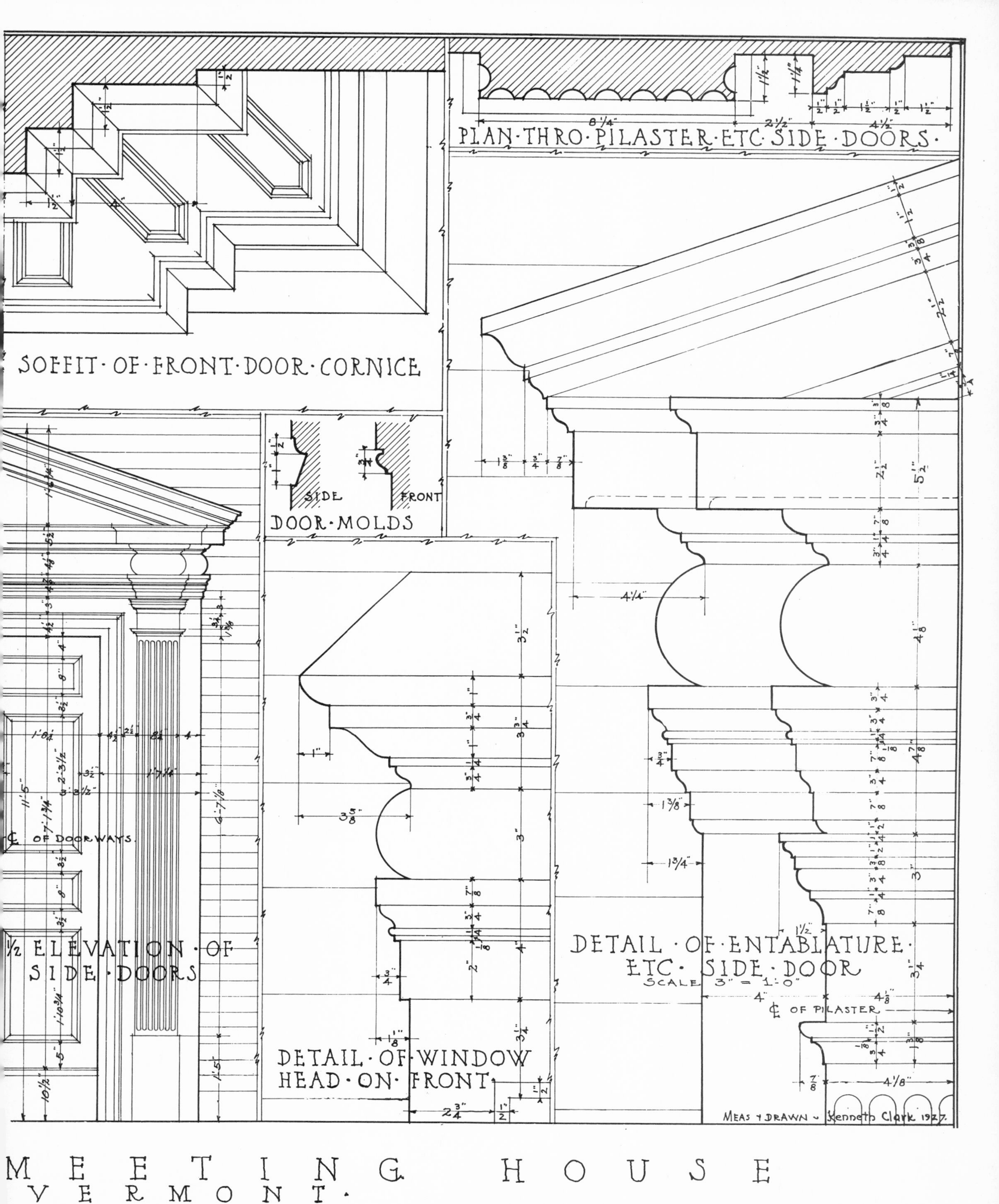


MEETING HOUSE

VERMONT ·

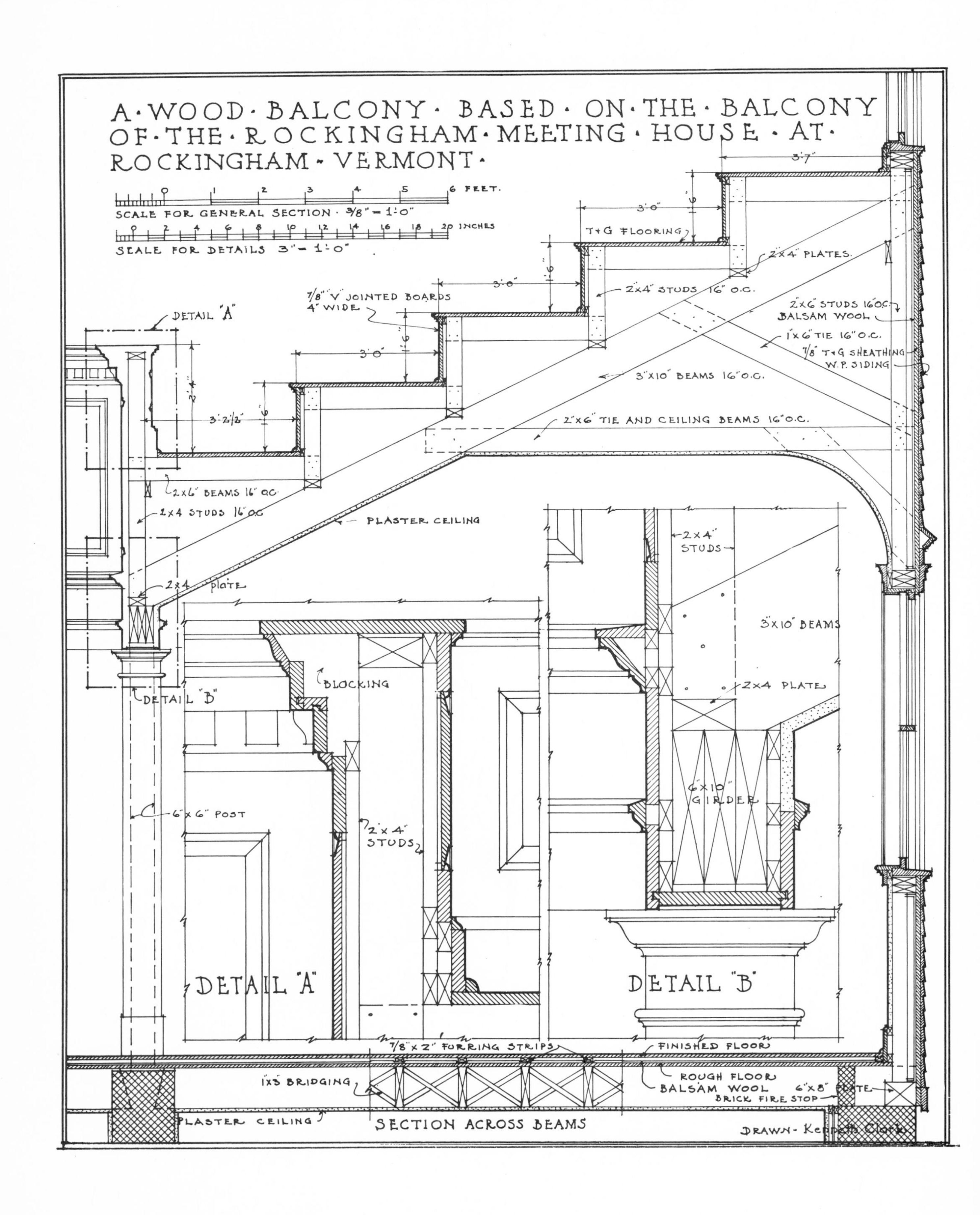
A·WOOD·BALCONY·BASED·ON·THE·BALCONY OF·THE·ROCKINGHAM·MEETING·HOUSE·AT· ROCKINGHAM·VERMONT·
0 1 2 3 4 5 6 FEET.
SCALE FOR GENERAL SECTION · 3/8" = 1'-0"
0 2 4 6 8 10 12 14 16 18 20 INCHES
SCALE FOR DETAILS 3" = 1'-0"
3'-7"
3'-0"
T+G FLOORING
2"x4" PLATES.
3'-0"
2"x4" STUDS 16" O.C.
7/8" V JOINTED BOARDS 4" WIDE
2"x6" STUDS 16" O.C.
BALSAM WOOL
1"x6" TIE 16" O.C.
7/8" T+G SHEATHING
W.P. SIDING
DETAIL "A"
3'-0"
3"x10" BEAMS 16" O.C.
3'-2 1/2"
2"x6" TIE AND CEILING BEAMS 16" O.C.
2x6" BEAMS 16" O.C.
2x4 STUDS 16" O.C.
PLASTER CEILING
2"x4" STUDS
2x4 plate
3"x10" BEAMS
BLOCKING
2x4 PLATE
DETAIL "B"
6"x10" GIRDER
6"x6" POST
2"x4" STUDS
DETAIL "A"
DETAIL "B"
7/8"x2" FURRING STRIPS
FINISHED FLOOR
ROUGH FLOOR
1x3 BRIDGING
BALSAM WOOL
6"x8" PLATE
BRICK FIRE STOP
PLASTER CEILING
SECTION ACROSS BEAMS
DRAWN - Kenneth Clark

INTERIOR OF ROCKINGHAM MEETING HOUSE, FROM THE GALLERY, ROCKINGHAM, VERMONT

CHURCH AT RICHMOND, VERMONT

*Richmond is in the Winooski River valley—between Burlington and Montpelier*

INTERIOR—CHURCH AT RICHMOND, VERMONT

*The columns are carved from one log from foundation to roof*

LOWER PART OF PULPIT—CHURCH AT RICHMOND, VERMONT

THE FROST FARM WITH GARRISON HOUSE AT REAR, EAST ELIOT, MAINE

THE MAJOR CHARLES FROST GARRISON HOUSE–1738–EAST ELIOT, MAINE *Plank Stairs and Door, Framing, etc.*

# New England Garrison Houses

The "Garrison House" of the Northern Colonies was a distinct type developed to meet the needs of the various communities scattered along the border in the period of the King Philip and the several French and Indian Wars. Except the brief unpleasantness, sometimes called the Pequot War, in 1637, and two short periods of Indian raiding in 1642 and '53, most of the local Indian tribes remained on friendly terms with the settlers, until 1675, when King Philip's War broke out in June, in Plymouth County, Massachusetts. This was the first occasion for any general provision being made to protect the lives of the settlers from human enemies, and its real seriousness is indicated by the fact that during the fighting of 1675 through 1677 over six hundred colonists lost their lives, and an even larger number of homes were burned and destroyed; a very considerable drain upon the population and prosperity of the Northern New England settlements at that time.

Following a dozen years of peace, another struggle began—often called King William's War—and continued from about 1688 or '90 to 1697 or '98. The Indians now came from farther afield, and were backed and instigated by the French in Canada. After a brief peace, from 1699 to 1703, Queen Anne's War broke out and waged until July of 1713, followed by another war with the French and Indians, known as Dummer's War, which lasted until the summer of 1726, when peace was signed at Falmouth (Portland) in the summer of that year and lasted for about twenty years. These same hostilities are, farther north, sometimes known as "Lovewell's War," and cost the colonies £170,000.

Deerfield, on the Connecticut River, is a well known example that shows, in the close clustering of its old houses along one short village street, the effect the Indian threat exerted upon its "community plan"!

Settled in 1669, the town street was laid out in 1671. Even as early as 1675, at the outbreak of the Indian Wars, it had a little over a hundred inhabitants, with Hadley and Brookfield, its nearest neighbors, nearly fifty miles away. In 1688 the town was partially fortified, and the Meeting House enclosed by a palisade. This palisade, or stockade, was a type of defense inherited from the Indians themselves. Within this area could be gathered the live stock as well as the human beings of the surrounding community. The limits of the stockade could include some brook, spring or well; and often even a part of the garden food supply. Within this enclosed area it was also customary to provide a strong "Blockhouse" or "Garrison" to shelter better the men, women, and children—giving them space to cook, eat, and sleep under something approaching normal conditions, while a few rough "penthouses" might be provided to help protect the farm stock.

The Garrison House ordinarily had two rooms to a floor and a chimney either in the center or at one or

GARRISON HOUSE—DR. PEASLEE—ROCK VILLAGE, MASSACHUSETTS

JOSEPH PEASLEE GARRISON–1675
–ROCK VILLAGE, MASS.

both ends. When the house was more than one story in height the upper walls might be of logs or plank. Sometimes the house had walls of only one story in height; sometimes there were two stories—in which case the upper always overhung the lower. The walls were built of heavy timber, cut to a usual seven inches thickness, ingeniously fitted together at the angles, and with musketry loopholes in the walls, and often one or two square "portholes" or shuttered openings about 12″ by 16″, or thereabouts, upon each front. The roofs seem to have been usually lightly built, with a heavily timbered floor in the attic which was always kept thoroughly covered with ashes or sand so that the lower part of the structure would be less apt to be ignited in case the Indians were able to set fire to the roof by means of their arrows.

*The Halliday Historic Photograph Co.*

"OLD INDIAN HOUSE" GARRISON, DEERFIELD, MASSACHUSETTS

Along the northern and western boundaries of the colonies the town records and histories are filled with references as to the methods taken to protect villages and homesteads, requiring all settlers to build only within limited distances of the Garrison Houses or Churches (the first churches were often built as community houses of defense, as well!). A few fortunate communities already had—or were soon to construct—houses of brick which, because of their better resistance to fire, were at once utilized as "Garrisons" or "houses of refuge" by those living nearby. Others arranged to have such houses built, or assisted in their construction, whenever possible, selecting locations upon raised hills or knolls conveniently central to some group of settlers or settlements.

An endeavor was made to have these "Garrisons" occur at regular and fairly close intervals along the boundaries of the occupied and settled lands, or near important fords and river crossings. Meanwhile the more protected Garrison Houses continued to be occupied, with the window openings enlarged, the walls clapboarded outside for better protection against weather, and plastered for more modern convenience within, until it soon became difficult to trace their older purposes.

Structures of this characteristic type were built even in comparatively late years, and in protected communities. For instance, a "watch-house" was built in Ipswich, near the Meeting House, as late as 1745; and two of the most interesting special buildings done for purposes of defense date from 1732 and 1738, and are still to be seen at Eliot, Maine; comparatively unchanged on the interior, though the exterior has been covered with clapboards and a large barn doorway cut through the closely matched logs of the larger in order to continue its usefulness and adapt it to the more profitable and peaceful pursuit of agriculture!

But these old "log garrisons" are the most indubitable and characteristic product of the problem and the times; the best examples of the architectural adaptation of local materials to a human need; the solution of the vital problem of providing "shelter"—in its most essential form—to the early inhabitants of the settlements in New England.

One of the oldest and most interesting of this group is the log garrison built at Exeter, N. H., by Councillor John Gilman probably between 1655 and '57. He settled in Exeter and in 1647 with his brother Edward built and operated a saw mill at "the Falls," a few

*Photo by W. S. Appleton, 1910*

DAM-DREW-ROUNDS GARRISON, DOVER, NEW HAMPSHIRE

*(Building Restored in 1917)*
THE HAZZEN-SPILLER GARRISON HOUSE—1724—HAVERHILL, MASSACHUSETTS

hundred feet from the house. By 1657 he had sawn out and built nearby a two-story house of oak timber seven inches thick. The first story had the logs tenoned into upright corner posts which upheld a bracketed girt, overhanging the first story about ten inches. The floor was laid across the house, using logs about six inches thick and often two feet wide, set close together; and this puncheon floor construction is still to be seen in one room of the dwelling. The second story wall was built of timber of the same thickness, but the corners were dovetailed together. The story heights were low (about 6′-6″), and if the structure originally had a central chimney, it has now disappeared. A staircase has replaced the probable early steep ladder, and evidence has existed that indicates the entrance doorway was originally protected by a sliding grill or portcullis.

By about 1750 Councillor Peter Gilman had built on an ell across the west end to entertain John Wentworth, the last of the Colonial Governors, and increased the new story heights by lowering the first floor almost two feet below the older portion and raising the second-floor ceiling. At the same time he carried the new cornice and exterior treatment entirely around the structure, raising a new roof above the old and making the top row of glass lights in the new fifteen-light second-story windows above the top of the older window openings in the old "garrison" portion of the building! A part of the plaster wall in the northwest corner room of the old Garrison, and also upon the newer stairway, has been removed so that the old timber wall of the early dwelling is exposed. The second-story room of the new ell is panelled on all four sides, although some of the rooms in the older portion contain panelled ends of earlier design and execution. In 1796, when Daniel Webster was fourteen years old and came to Exeter to study at the Academy, he lived in the rooms in the second floor, northwest corner, of the Garrison part of the dwelling, which was then known as the "Clifford" house. Another Garrison stood a short distance away on "the plains," the Janvrin Garrison, built in 1680 or earlier, but it has been so changed as to have lost all its old character. It had "planked walls."

In the Woodman Institute, at Dover, may still be seen the old Dam-Drew Garrison House, which was built by William Dam, son of Deacon John Dam, in 1675, in the "Back River" District in Dover Neck, about three miles south of Dover. It was removed to its present location in 1916. It is a one-story squared-log structure, 42′ by 24′6″, with a foot-wide overhang, carrying an 8″ by 19″ projecting plate against which the rafters rest. It was occupied continuously until after the Civil War, when the weather began to get at the pins and corner notches (which were not cut on a slope to throw out the rain, as in most structures of this type). Hackmatack seems to have been the principal material from which the logs were squared. The chimney has been rebuilt —of smaller bricks than the original—but the interior partitions and arrangement have been retained, so that the visitor may here obtain as good an idea of the Garrison log type as it is now possible to secure. Both the loopholes, and small openings about 10″ by 12″, are easily found.

THE NATHANIEL PEASLEE GARRISON HOUSE—1675-80 —WEST NEWBURY, MASSACHUSETTS

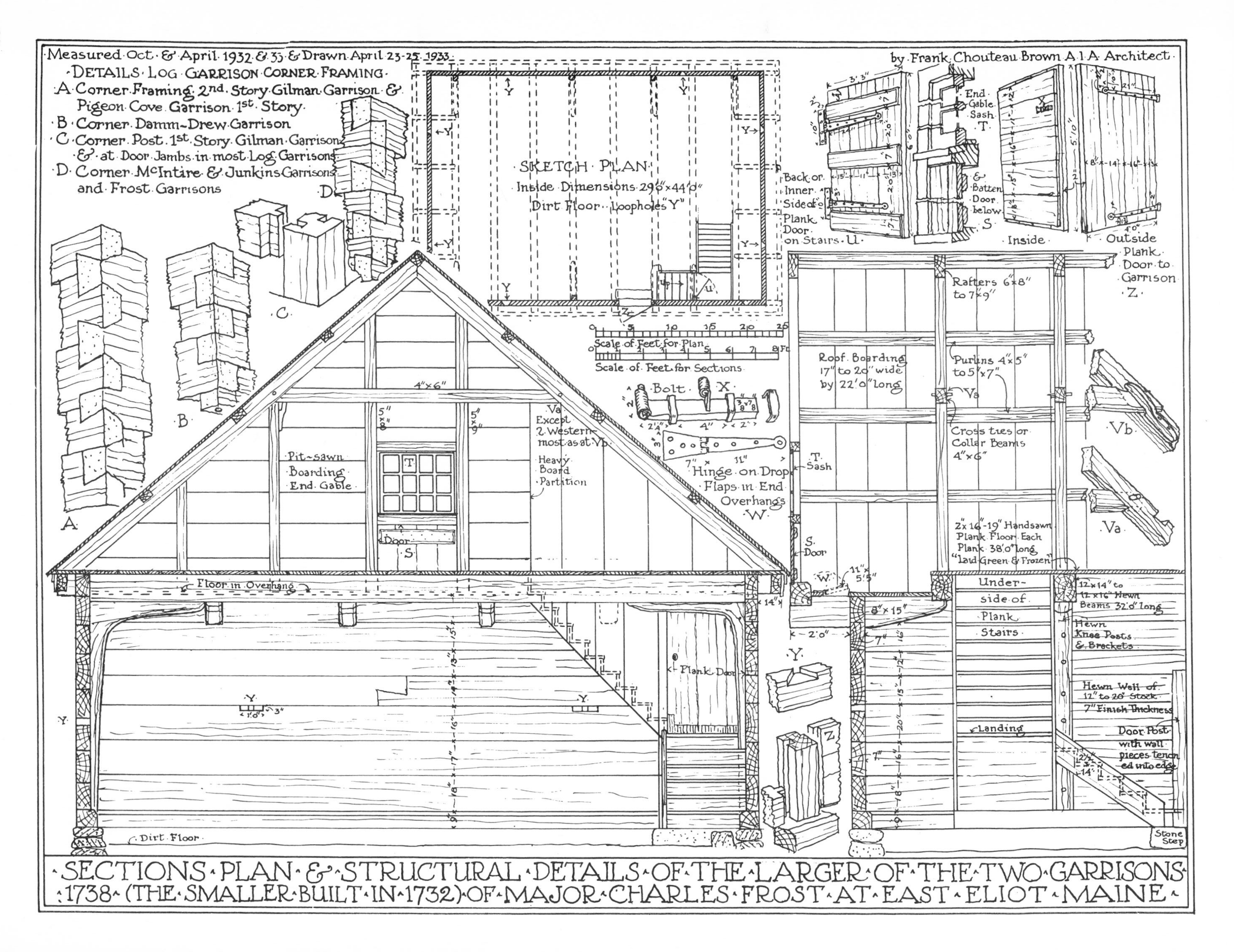

Measured Oct. & April 1932 & 33 & Drawn April 23-25 1933.
DETAILS LOG GARRISON CORNER FRAMING
A Corner Framing 2nd Story Gilman Garrison & Pigeon Cove Garrison 1st Story
B Corner Damm-Drew Garrison
C Corner Post 1st Story Gilman Garrison & at Door Jambs in most Log Garrisons
D Corner McIntire & Junkins Garrisons and Frost Garrisons
by Frank Chouteau Brown A.I.A. Architect
SKETCH PLAN
Inside Dimensions 29'6"x44'0"
Dirt Floor Loopholes "Y"
Scale of Feet for Plan
Scale of Feet for Sections
Back or Inner Side of Plank Door on Stairs U
End Gable Sash T
& Batten Door below S
Inside
Outside Plank Door to Garrison Z
Rafters 6"x8" to 7"x9"
Purlins 4"x5" to 5"x7"
Roof Boarding 17" to 20" wide by 22'0" Long
Cross ties or Collar Beams 4"x6"
Bolt
X
Hinge on Drop Flaps in End Overhangs W
T Sash
S Door
2"x 16"-19" Handsawn Plank Floor Each Plank 38'0" Long "laid Green & Frozen"
12"x14" to 12"x16" Hewn Beams 32'0" Long
Hewn Knee Posts & Brackets
Under-side of Plank Stairs
Landing
Hewn Wall of 12" to 20" Stock 7" Finish Thickness
Door Post with wall pieces tenoned into edge
Stone Step
Pit-sawn Boarding End Gable
Va Except 2 Western-most as at Vb
Heavy Board Partition
Floor in Overhang
Plank Door
Dirt Floor
SECTIONS PLAN & STRUCTURAL DETAILS OF THE LARGER OF THE TWO GARRISONS 1738 (THE SMALLER BUILT IN 1732) OF MAJOR CHARLES FROST AT EAST ELIOT MAINE

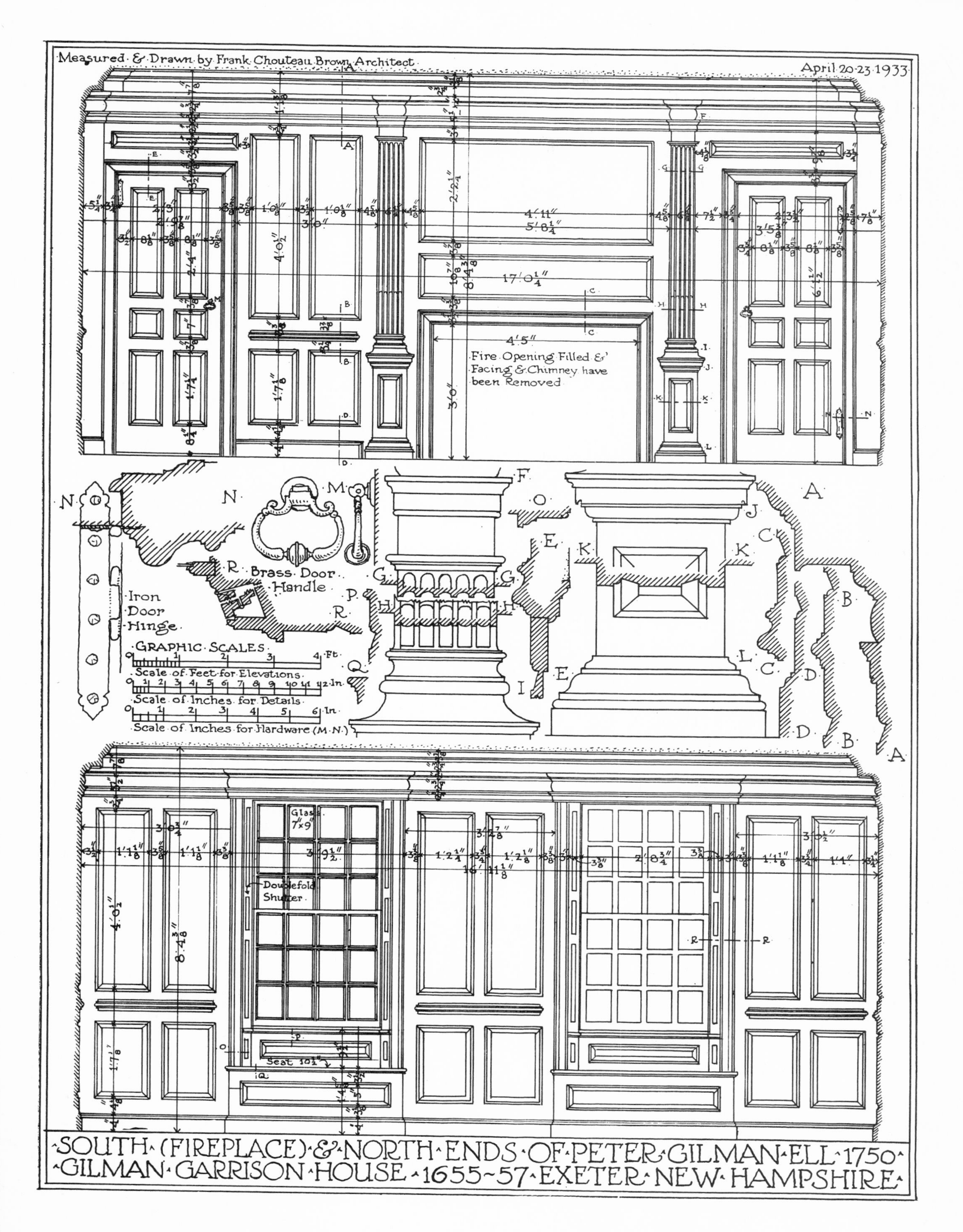
Measured & Drawn by Frank Chouteau Brown Architect
April 20-23 1933
Fire Opening Filled & Facing & Chimney have been Removed
Brass Door Handle
Iron Door Hinge
GRAPHIC SCALES
Scale of Feet for Elevations
Scale of Inches for Details
Scale of Inches for Hardware (M-N)
Glass 7"x9"
Doublefold Shutter
Seat
SOUTH (FIREPLACE) & NORTH ENDS OF PETER GILMAN ELL 1750
GILMAN GARRISON HOUSE 1655~57 EXETER NEW HAMPSHIRE

*Original Log Garrison Portion at Left. The 1750 Wing Shows Projected Beyond at Right.*

PETER GILMAN ELL–1750–GILMAN GARRISON HOUSE, EXETER, NEW HAMPSHIRE

*Log Post or External Corner Angle of First Floor Framing. The Lower Part of 2nd Story Corner Framing (Dovetailed) Appears at Upper Right-hand Corner.*

*Inside of Exterior Corner, 2nd Floor Room. The Log in Which the Square Opening is Cut is About 21" High x 7" Thick. Sawn Log Faces Were Later Hacked to Hold Plaster.*

THE GILMAN GARRISON HOUSE—1655-57—EXETER, NEW HAMPSHIRE

*Rear View of Original Log Garrison Portion.*

*Only One of the Old Windows Remains in the Attic of the Front Gable.*

DUSTON GARRISON HOUSE —1696-97—HAVERHILL, MASS.

The large Garrison was evidently intended to accommodate animals as well as human beings, and the perfection of the smooth hewn log surfaces, their close fit at the joints, both horizontal and end joinings, as well as the tightness of the pit-sawn plank floor, "laid green and frozen," are most remarkable today.

This section was especially open to Indian raids, and many Garrisons were maintained here during the later years of the French and Indian wars. In 1695, twenty Garrisons were listed in Durham as being maintained by the authorities, and each soldier cost the Province at the rate of £3, s.12, d.0 board for eighteen weeks, according to the old records, while from one to four soldiers were quartered in each of the Garrisons.

Another two-story garrison nearby, the Bunker Garrison , was 40′-6″ by 20′-9″, and the corner angles were notched, and the door posts had logs tenoned into them, while the top of the low doorway was cut into a slight segment of an arch in the under edge of the caplog.

There are many old brick Garrisons in this northern section, some of which were originally built with that purpose in mind, and others adapted to it as being the "most defensible" in their locality.

Thomas Duston, who had settled in Kittery in 1654, afterwards removed to the top of a hill outside Haverhill—then Pentucket—where he experimented in making bricks, finally building the present house of them some time during 1696-97, with "floors and roof of white oak."

Haverhill, Massachusetts, occupied an important point on what remained the northern frontier of the New England colonies for nearly seventy years. The town records of 1690 show the appointment of six Garrison houses, and four "houses of refuge."

In describing the characteristics of the houses located in that vicinity, Mirick writes: "Most of the garrisons and two of the houses of refuge—those belonging to Joseph and Nathaniel Peaslee—were built of brick, and were two stories high; those that were not built of this material had a single laying of it between the outer and the inner walls. They had but one outside door, which was often so small that but one person could enter at a time; their windows were about two feet and a half in length, eighteen inches in breadth, and were secured on the inside with iron bars. Their glass was very small, cut in the shape of a diamond, was extremely thick, and fastened in with lead instead of putty. There were generally but two rooms in the basement (first) story, and tradition says that they entered the chamber with the help of a ladder instead of stairs so that the inmates could retreat into them and take it up if the basement-story should be taken by the enemy. Their fireplaces were of such enormous sizes that they could burn their wood, sled-length, very conveniently, and the ovens opened on the outside of the building, generally at one end."

This description well applies to the Hazzen-Spiller house, a listed Garrison, built in 1724, about three-quarters of a mile below the center of the town.

The Dickenson-Pillsbury-Witham House, built on a knoll beside the road in Georgetown, near the Rowley line, previous to 1700, is described in an early family record, as follows: "It was built in the time of the Indian depredations. My great-grandmother occupied it in the time of the Indians. It was lined from the sill to the girth with bricks between the plastering and the boards. There were doors outside the windows to shut at night. The outside doors were barred inside. One night the Indians came and attacked the house, making an attempt to cut the outside (doors) down to get into the house. My great-grandmother took a pail of scalding water, went upstairs, and poured it onto their heads, and they were glad to retire." J. L. Ewell, in his *Story of Byfield, a New England Parish,* further adds: "In these houses, the second story frequently projected over the lower one for defense against the Indian, and the roof ran down to the lower story in the rear, making a back 'linter' (lean-to). In the huge chimney was the bench where the family could sit cozily and watch the great fire of logs or read by its light. Mr. Witham's house is probably an heirloom from the seventeenth century. Its architecture closely resembles that of the old house on Kent's Island, not now standing, that was said to have been built in 1653. The large living room has a huge fireplace in which two cook-stoves stand side by side, a beautifully carved wooden latch on the great cellar door, a crane five or six feet long attached to a great beam in the ceiling to swing out and hold candlesticks suspended by trammels and wooden partitions dressed of old with blue clay and skim milk in lieu of paint." This original surfacing can still be seen on portions of the woodwork in this room shown below.

Paul Pillsbury, one of its inhabitants, in the war of 1812, shouldered and carried a cannon weighing seven hundred pounds. He invented in this house the "peg machine" that revolutionized the shoe business in New England, selling pegs for eight cents a quart or $2.00 a bushel—that formerly had to be painfully split and whittled by hand out of maple by the shoe makers. The first cut nails were also made nearby, in a factory on the Parker River, where were also the first cotton and woolen mills in America, dating from 1636, and the first fulling mill, from 1643.

THE McINTIRE GARRISON HOUSE—1640-45
—SCOTLAND, NEAR YORK, MAINE

THE DICKENSON-PILLSBURY-WITHAM
GARRISON HOUSE—1700—GEORGETOWN, MASS.

HOUSE AT 43 MEETING HOUSE HILL, PORTSMOUTH, NEW HAMPSHIRE.
**Detail of Doorway.**

# Portsmouth, New Hampshire

ANNO DOMINI 1630 saw the beginnings of Portsmouth. Twenty years after the first permanent settlement at Jamestown, and but ten years after the landing of the Pilgrims at Plymouth Rock, John Mason and his associates sailed into Portsmouth Harbor and established upon its shore the first settlement of the New Hampshire colony. No mere chance determined the site. The wooded and gently sloping shore of this beautiful and convenient harbor affording a safe haven for sailing craft on a "storm and rock-bound coast," was a logical selection. From a collection of a few small huts, the town grew and increased in importance for two hundred years. Time was when Portsmouth bid fair to be a commercial rival of New York, and in the early centuries of American history its part is written large upon the record. It reached the zenith of its development in the first years of the nineteenth century, but the invention of the steamboat and the coming of the iron-hulled deep-draft vessel marked the beginning of the end of Portsmouth's commercial supremacy. While from that time Portsmouth does not seem to have gone noticeably forward, perhaps because of the beauty of its location and the healthfulness of its climate, or because the Government continued to maintain there an important naval station, it nevertheless does not seem to have gone backward. It is to-day no decayed nor deserted city, but one which has seemed to hold miraculously unchanged the quiet and romantic character that it possessed as the home of many of the best and most distinguished citizens of our late Colonial and early Republican periods.

To the architect and the historian the city of Portsmouth makes a special appeal. Other towns have retained much of their early flavor, but in none of them, as in Portsmouth, do we have a whole community the character of which has not really changed for a century. The summer tourist may think of Portsmouth only as a railway center from which he passes to Rye Beach or the Isles of Shoals, and remember alone the orange cake for which one of its modest confectioneries is noted; but to one whose eyes are open and whose mind is attuned to the memories with which its streets and docks and homes are filled, this old town has an enduring charm. For this ancient metropolis played a stirring part in our early history. It was here the expedition started which captured Louisburg, and high in the steeple of old St. John's Church still hangs the bell that pealed over that early capital of New France. Paul Revere was no stranger to the New Hampshire town, and an earlier ride of his, not chronicled in verse, provided powder and shot used at Lexington and Bunker Hill. Here lived Governor Langdon, that stalwart patriot who pledged all his money and a warehouse of Jamaica rum to provide uniforms and arms for Stark's Continentals, who at Bennington won lasting fame and saved Mollie Stark from widowhood. The docks of Portsmouth were no less familiar to John Paul Jones than the quarter-deck of the *Bonhomme Richard,* and on foggy nights his spirit and those of a galaxy of other gallant heroes still wend their way through its well-loved streets to the Yard. When the moon is just right you can see them: Hull of the *Constitution,* Decatur, Bainbridge, and the gallant Lawrence, and after they have passed, great men of a later day,—Franklin Pierce and Daniel

THE JACOB WENDELL HOUSE, PORTSMOUTH, NEW HAMPSHIRE.
Built in 1789 by Jeremiah Hill.

Webster, and a host of others. There are memories here, too, of statesmen of our own generation who met and signed the treaty which ended the Russo-Japanese War. Portsmouth has played no mean part in history, but, after all, it is not that which holds for us its greatest interest. It is because it stands to-day, just as it stood more than a hundred years ago, simple and unostentatious, and yet clearly the home of an early American "Four Hundred." There is an atmosphere of elegance and refinement in the old city of Portsmouth not found often in America. The wealth of many other Colonial towns is physically more evident. Portsmouth has no street of wealthy "nabobs" like Chestnut Street in Salem; and even to such a discerning eye as that of George Washington, when he visited Portsmouth after his inauguration, the pine-built homes of Portsmouth seemed "inconsiderable," compared to the brick mansions of Virginia. But these houses stand to-day a unique record of a civilization and a culture which must have been very gentle and very fine. They are still full of exquisite furniture and china which are the envy of collectors; portraits by Copley and other distinguished painters abound, and help us in imagination to see those gentlewomen of that early day with powdered hair and flowing silks, Colonial governors and other imposing dignitaries in velvets, young blades in knee-breeches and satin waistcoats, dining tables groaning under their weight of damask and silver, fine wines in glittering decanters, and the rarest of china from the Orient.

It is a snug and well built city. Twice or three times fire had swept across it, and, rebuilt, it seems to have been each time better than before. Not a city of great mansions with outbuildings for slaves and other retainers, but a city of homes of high-bred, God-fearing gentlemen; for if architecture can record, as it surely does, the character of a people, it writes large in Portsmouth the refinement and gentility of that early town.

HOUSE AT 363 STATE STREET,
PORTSMOUTH, NEW HAMPSHIRE.

THE BUCKMINSTER HOUSE,
PORTSMOUTH, NEW HAMPSHIRE.
Built in 1720 by Daniel Warner.

THE GOVERNOR LANGDON HOUSE, PORTSMOUTH, NEW HAMPSHIRE
Built in 1784.

HOUSE AT 124 PLEASANT STREET, PORTSMOUTH, NEW HAMPSHIRE.

Nowhere as here was the three-story American house of wood so successfully and consistently developed. The Haven house, built about 1800, with its well designed fence, after the manner of McIntyre in Salem; the Governor Woodbury mansion, built in 1809 by Samuel Ham; the Langley Boardman house, with its charming palladian window and delightful semicircular porch, its unique mahogany door paneled with oval inserts or moldings in whalebone; the Ladd, or Moffit, house, with its magnificent interiors; and last, but not least, the John Pierce house on Court Street, with its well designed façade, its delightful stairway, and interesting plan, are all distinguished examples of this unusual type.

It is characteristic of Portsmouth that its houses are essentially city houses, and not, as in so many other places, suburban dwellings swallowed up by the city. It is characteristic, too, of Portsmouth that, with but three important exceptions, its houses are uniformly of wood.

We are apt to remember of most of our New England towns, a few houses of special architectural merit which stand out against a background of others of the simplest character; but in Portsmouth the standard of all the houses is so high that it is a virtue that our illustrations are taken from the rank and file of its early buildings rather than those of outstanding merit. Some of the most charming of them are of the Wendell house, built by Jeremiah Hill at the cor-

THE TREADWELL HOUSE, PORTSMOUTH, NEW HAMPSHIRE. Built in 1750.

THE JACOB WENDELL HOUSE, PORTSMOUTH, NEW HAMPSHIRE.
Entrance Detail—Built in 1789.

THE GOVERNOR BENNING WENTWORTH HOUSE,
LITTLE HARBOR, PORTSMOUTH, NEW HAMPSHIRE.
Built in 1750.

ner of Edward and Pleasant streets. Its exterior is of clapboards set a few inches to the weather, like so many other houses of northern New England. It is delightful in mass as well as in detail. The door, of twelve panels, beautifully designed, carries, it would seem, the original knocker and an ancient door-plate, while in the broken pediment above is set a most interesting feature consisting of a whale-oil lamp carved in wood, set upon an ornamental base, suggesting the source of the wealth of its original owner. A close examination of the detailed photograph will discover a repetition of the lamp motif in the pediments of the dormers. It is interesting to find this record of the owner embodied in the architecture of his house, and a pity it is, that one so seldom finds such a personal note. It is a pleasing indication of the early interest of architect and owner in the details of its construction; but wherever one turns in a careful study of this modest and unassuming structure there is found the evidence of the affectionate interest of its designer.

House on Livermore Street.

Notice such seemingly unimportant things as the moldings at the chimney-caps, the sweep and proportion of the granite steps and copings, the height and the detail of the iron posts and rails. It would have been so easy to have made the railing of the usual and accepted height, and to have missed the scale which it lends to the whole composition.

The little house at 314 Court Street is of piquant interest. The frame of the entrance door is delightfully original and interesting, but it is terribly marred in its effect by the modern door and transom within it. How many architects have passed this house and wished that they might have the courage to ring the bell and ask its history, or to suggest the pleasure that it would give them to set inside that charming frame a door and fanlight which would be in keeping!

The houses at 124 Pleasant Street; Livermore Street; and the Samuel Lord House are quite of the general run of Portsmouth's houses. They are simple, straightforward buildings, two windows flanking on each side an interesting doorway in the first story, and with five windows across the front in the second, the roof being hipped or gambreled, as the case may be, and, in the case of the Lord House now occupied by the

TWO DOORWAYS AT
PORTSMOUTH, NEW HAMPSHIRE.

House at 314 Court Street.

THE SAMUEL LORD HOUSE, PORTSMOUTH, NEW HAMPSHIRE.
Built in 1730 by Captain Purcell. The home of
John Paul Jones during his stay in Portsmouth.

Portsmouth Historical Society, pierced with dormers. This house, historically as well as architecturally, is the most important of the three, as it was the home of John Paul Jones during his residence in Portsmouth.

The fence and fence-posts for all these houses are well designed, and recall those built in Salem during the same period. Those who planned them had no hesitancy in combining carefully cut granite bases and steps with wood fences and posts. It is of value to note that though built more than a hundred years ago, the work in wood shows no greater signs of decay than the New Hampshire granite itself. The house at 363 State Street has a latter-day American basement effect, with its steps and entrance door recessed within the front wall. The Doric columns of its addition and the slight modifications in its detail would indicate that it was made some years after the building of the original house.

There is something delightfully satisfying about the old house on Meeting House Hill, and it is valuable to analyze its charm. It seems to consist in the fine texture given by the close-spaced clapboards, the studied disposition of windows and doors, together with the charming detail of its window heads, entrance door, and trim. It should be an incentive to the architectural draftsman of to-day to realize how much genuine pleasure there is in the contemplation of this studied, but simple, building. It is the sort of thing "anybody could do," yet almost nobody can. It has the qualities of great monumental architecture—correct proportion, simplicity, and interest.

The Governor Langdon house, though not the largest, is perhaps the most pretentious of the wood houses of Portsmouth. We can believe that no money was spared in its construction, and it has suffered from the consequent over-richness of its design. Its Corinthian capitals are marvels of wood-carving and of preserva-

HOUSE AT 271 COURT STREET, PORTSMOUTH, NEW HAMPSHIRE.
Entrance Detail.

tion. This was the home of the early Governor of New Hampshire who pledged his means for the Continental cause, and within its walls have been entertained admirals, generals, and world-renowned statesmen of more than one generation.

The Wentworth-Gardner house stands upon a terrace shaded by a magnificent linden, and looks out across beautiful Portsmouth Harbor.

Its location is in a section of the town which perhaps most shows its age.

A purist might criticize the design of the facade, made as it is in wood in imitation of stone ashlar, but might well pardon its architect when he studies its delightful proportions and details, both in exterior and interior. The house as photographed is not quite as it was built. Some of its interest is due to the fascinating doorway with scrolled pediment and gilded pineapple applied by its recent owner. There are not many towns where there is anything much finer than the interior of this house.

Thus ends our little glimpse of this ancient metropolis. There is so much more to be said, and so much there to be seen, that this ending, like that of school, should be but the commencement. For the student of American architecture no sojourn will be happier or of more lasting value than the time he spends in this delightful city.

THE WENTWORTH-GARDNER HOUSE, PORTSMOUTH, NEW HAMPSHIRE.
Built in 1760.

THE COLONEL ROBERT MEANS HOUSE, AMHERST, NEW HAMPSHIRE

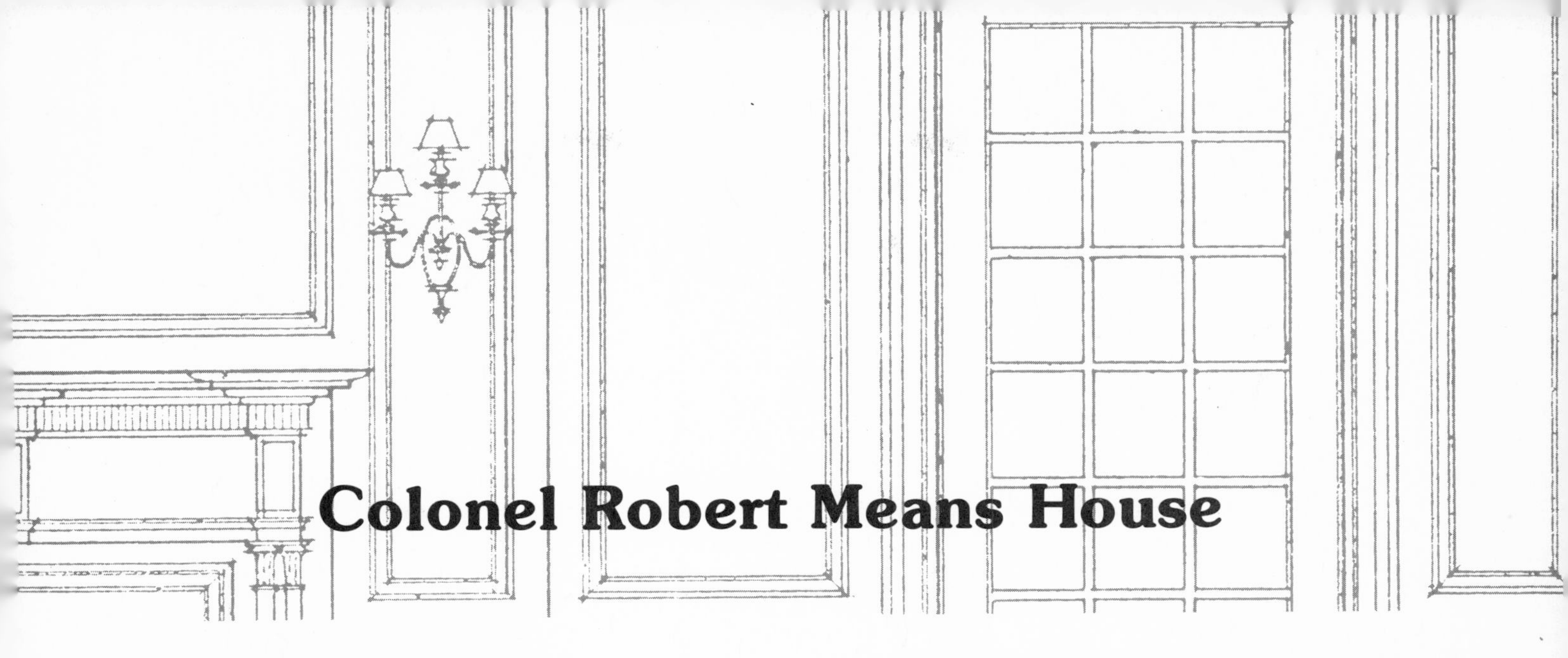

# Colonel Robert Means House

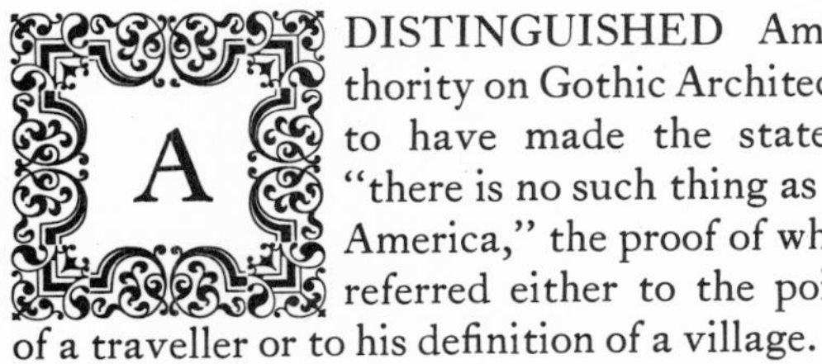

A DISTINGUISHED American authority on Gothic Architecture is said to have made the statement that "there is no such thing as a village in America," the proof of which may be referred either to the point of view of a traveller or to his definition of a village.

If he looks for a picturesque huddle of houses with quaint broken lines and interesting textures of masonry and roof such as delights our eyes in Europe the statement is correct.

If, on the contrary, he consults a dictionary he will find the following definition, "Village,—a small assemblage of houses, less than a town or city and larger than a hamlet." With this idea in mind anyone who has travelled in this country will find here and there in the older States and particularly in New England a few such "assemblages" as yet unspoiled and with picturesque qualities of their own.

Such a village is Amherst, New Hampshire, not exactly off the beaten track, for a tarred and numbered road runs through it and so do automobiles with license plates of remote States. There are electric lights and the general store and garage have gasoline for sale; but the woodbine twining around the electric light poles seems to give a symbolic suggestion of its real aloofness from the world.

The location of the town has a good deal to do with this and goes to prove that environment is stronger than heredity. Originally, it was the Shire town of Hillsborough County as its disused Courthouse shows, but now business has slipped away to the valley of the Merrimack, which flows seven miles to the east turning the wheels of many mills, and has carried the Courts with it.

To the south, the railroad follows the valley of the Souhegan winding among the foothills of the Temple Mountains—that beautiful range which veils Monadnock from the Merrimack and tempts summer visitors to regions of wilder and more extended views than from "Amherst Plain" as the "Common" is called.

The village, however, has the advantage of its defects. The trolley car has avoided it and it has not a tea-room,—a gift-shop,—nor a hot dog stand. Since the abandonment of the branch railroad which once came discreetly to its outskirts, the would-be tourist who has no motor must take a "bus" which leaves him three miles from the Centre.

Hence it is that it has kept its charm, a bit of Cranford in New England looking almost as it did in the days when it was a social and legal centre.

It must be a full quarter of a mile from the Spaulding House at the West end of the "Plain" to the brick Courthouse which faces it at the other end with the old graveyard behind it. And on either side besides the church, the public library, and the two stores are houses, each in its own large yard. Most of them are white with green blinds, some of them unimportant but there is not a "French Roof" among them. And the "Plain" and the houses on it and on the side streets which radiate from it are overhung with beautiful trees culminating in a solemn group of pines in the graveyard.

Near the Courthouse and the graveyard and cut off from the main road by a stretch of greensward bearing a magnificent elm stands the house which Colonel Robert Means built in 1785 (Monday, May 30, was "the raising").

Robert Means was born in Ireland in 1742. He was a weaver by trade and came to Boston with a friend in 1766. They first settled in Merrimack, carrying their wares about the country in their packs. It is astounding to find that their business increased so that they decided to establish another trade centre at Amherst. Neither wanting to go, they tossed up for it and so Robert Means came to Amherst about 1774 bringing his young wife with him and here he lived until his death in 1823. At first he carried on his trade of weaving but later devoted himself to the mercantile side of the business keeping a sort of general store next to the house. By integrity and ability he amassed what was a large fortune for those times and had a position of high

THE EAST WALL OF THE PARLOR (NORTHWEST ROOM) FIRST FLOOR

THE HALL AND STAIRWAY

social as well as financial standing. He was a member of the Legislature and held various offices, among them that of Colonel of Militia.

A year before Colonel Robert Means came to Amherst came Joshua Atherton, a lawyer and graduate of Harvard College with his wife and child. Between these men a life-long friendship sprang up. Their families intermarried and have been closely connected for over one hundred years.

After the Colonel's death his widow seems to have either sold or rented the house and for some twenty years it was occupied by outsiders. Robert Means, Jr. who had married Abigail Kent, the grandchild of Joshua Atherton, died in 1842 in Lowell where he had been superintendent of the Suffolk Mills. There were no children and his widow returned to Amherst and bought the old house. In it she established her mother and her brother George Kent and his wife.

It was her mother, Mrs. Amos Kent, who installed upon the staircase landing the busts of two of her brothers-in-law, their heads at their proper heights from the floor,—the Honorable Jeremiah Mason, six feet seven inches tall, the Honorable Amos Lawrence, about five feet four inches tall.

She died in 1846 but George Kent and his wife lived there until his death in 1883 and there their only child Anna Kent was born. Mrs. Robert Means, Jr. left the house to her sister, Mrs. James MacGregor, to go after her death to Anna Kent now Mrs. Charles Theodore Carruth and to her son after her.

Wholly without pretense, the house stands with quiet dignity under the locust trees behind the white fence which gives it an old fashioned privacy disdained by many modern communities.

It is a four square house with two chimneys, an ell with shed and barn parallel to the street giving it a long pleasing line. It is a very good New England example of the Second Period of Colonial Architecture,—the windows in pairs on either side of the front door, the latter hospitably wide, three panels wide, with fluted pilasters and a pediment with consoles.

In the center of each of the three other sides of the house is a similar doorway, that on the East being frankly an architectural decoration.

The hip roof, a little steeper than is usually found in this type is unbroken save at the South end where two dormers light the third story. This roof originally had a railing just above the dormers as is shown by an old engraving in the possession of the present owner.

The main cornice which has both consoles and dentils breaks around the second story window frames, the consoles being a little more closely spaced across them. As if to justify this, there is a half console placed in profile against the fascia on each side of each window.

The interior is of charming proportions, distinctly domestic,—the hall and staircase unusually beautiful, the latter recalling in its easy rise and tread that of the Lee Mansion in Marblehead though there is nothing grandiose about it. The balusters are turned and there are sawed stair ends. Beneath the stairs above the landing is a large panel with carved rosettes in the corners and below this there is a delightful vista through the wide garden door. The back staircase in the little hall between the two south rooms is also suggestive of the back staircase in the Lee Mansion and runs up two flights giving access to the "attic."

There is but one room in the main house which has not some interesting panelling. Six of them have panelled chimney breasts and some of them wainscot like that in the hall with chair rails at the level of the window stools. In two of the bedrooms the over mantel is inset an inch between the end pieces instead of projecting.

To the parlor, of course, was given the greatest consideration. Here we have the pilaster treatment, the cornice breaking around the capitals as it also does around the window heads. But where have we before met a moulding like that around the fireplace,—a small bolection moulding with ears and one carved member? And how exquisitely has Colonel Means suggested the solution of the problem of a mantel shelf with such a composition of fireplace and panel! The top member is, of course, a modern addition probably made by Abby Atherton Means.

As frequently happens in houses of this period, the windows in this, the best room, are recessed with seats and panelled shutters, the walls being thickened to get this effect which seems to have been purely decorative. Shutters which occur on every window on the ground floor, being probably intended for protection at night, are applied to some of the windows so as to swing clear into the room. In the sitting-room they slide into pockets in the wall and are fastened with brass pegs kept hanging by the sides of the windows. The panelled recess and seat, but without shutters, is found again on the landing of the stairs where there is a well proportioned arched window.

It is worthy of note that while the front and rear doors and the windows over them are centered on the house, they are not centered on the hall. This is because the sitting-room on the right of the hall is larger than the parlor on the left. The result is that from the entrance door there is a good view of the window on the landing.

THE COLONEL ROBERT MEANS HOUSE, AMHERST, NEW HAMPSHIRE

LANDING ON MAIN STAIRWAY

WINDOW ON STAIR LANDING

THE SOUTH FRONT

The fourth room on the ground floor now used as a dining room was the original kitchen. It is sheathed with wide pine boards, somewhat after the fashion of the First Period; these have never been painted. There Mrs. Abigail Atherton Kent Means did one dastardly deed. She took out the brick oven on the right-hand side of the fireplace. Cooking stoves had come in,—why take up so much room with an obsolete oven when the space it occupied gave such a useful closet with a slide through to the closet in the dining room? The enormous hearth is still there to show where it stood. Let us be grateful to her that least she replaced it with a six-panelled door like the others in the room. We certainly owe her a debt of gratitude for moving away Colonel Means' shop which was a large two-story building, both shop and warehouse, which stood close to the south side of the house at the front.

But it was no part of Colonel Means' plan to have a joyless, cheerless house. He was famed for his hospitality and to Amherst in its prime came many lawyers when Court was in session who were glad to find relaxation in the intervals of their professional duties in the society of the gay little town. Dances and card parties were frequent, the old letters tell us. So in the second story the wall between the hall and the bedroom, over the large sitting-room, is handsomely panelled and hinged at the top so that it may be hooked up to make a ballroom. This arrangement was a simple proposition in a house framed after the fashion of the Eighteenth century with self-supporting floors on which owners erected partitions where they chose.

Such is the Means house architecturally. It has, however, an unusual quality, an atmosphere, from the fact that for nearly eighty years it has been lived in by one family. It has been kept up but there has been a minimum of change or "restoration" and no dilapidation.

What Robert Means' furniture was like, we do not know. It went out with his wife and was probably scattered among his children. Some of it may have come back with his daughter-in-law. The house is as it was furnished in 1846. A purist, therefore, would wish to have many things "done over" as many of the furnishings especially the carpets are "Victorian." Anyone who demands "period" furniture will be disappointed.

The fact is, however, that the mellowness and quaintness of the furnishings give the house more expression than if it were absolutely true to form. It seems full of the gentle lives that have been lived there.

The "modern conveniences"—plumbing, electric lights, heating, etc., have been added with affectionate care and effort not to spoil the effect and so have the up-to-date ornaments and accessories of furniture. They have all been introduced with an almost Ruskin-like feeling of necessity and have taken their places in the house as has the moss on the trees about it or the little ferns in the cracks of the bricks in the front walk, as part of the bloom of the whole.

Especially must be mentioned the wall papers in the hall and parlor, of date unknown, faded and stained, and yet so unusual and attractive that it would seem a sacrilege to change them.

And as we look at all the refinements of the finish even at some of its naiveties and crudities, we wonder where and how the weaver who peddled his goods about the country learned how to choose his proportions and details so wisely.

THE EAST ELEVATION

THE NORTHEAST ROOM—FIRST FLOOR

# *The* COLONEL ROBERT MEANS HOUSE AMHERST, NEW HAMPSHIRE

MEASURED DRAWINGS *from The George F. Lindsay Collection*

DETAIL OF GATE AND ENTRANCE

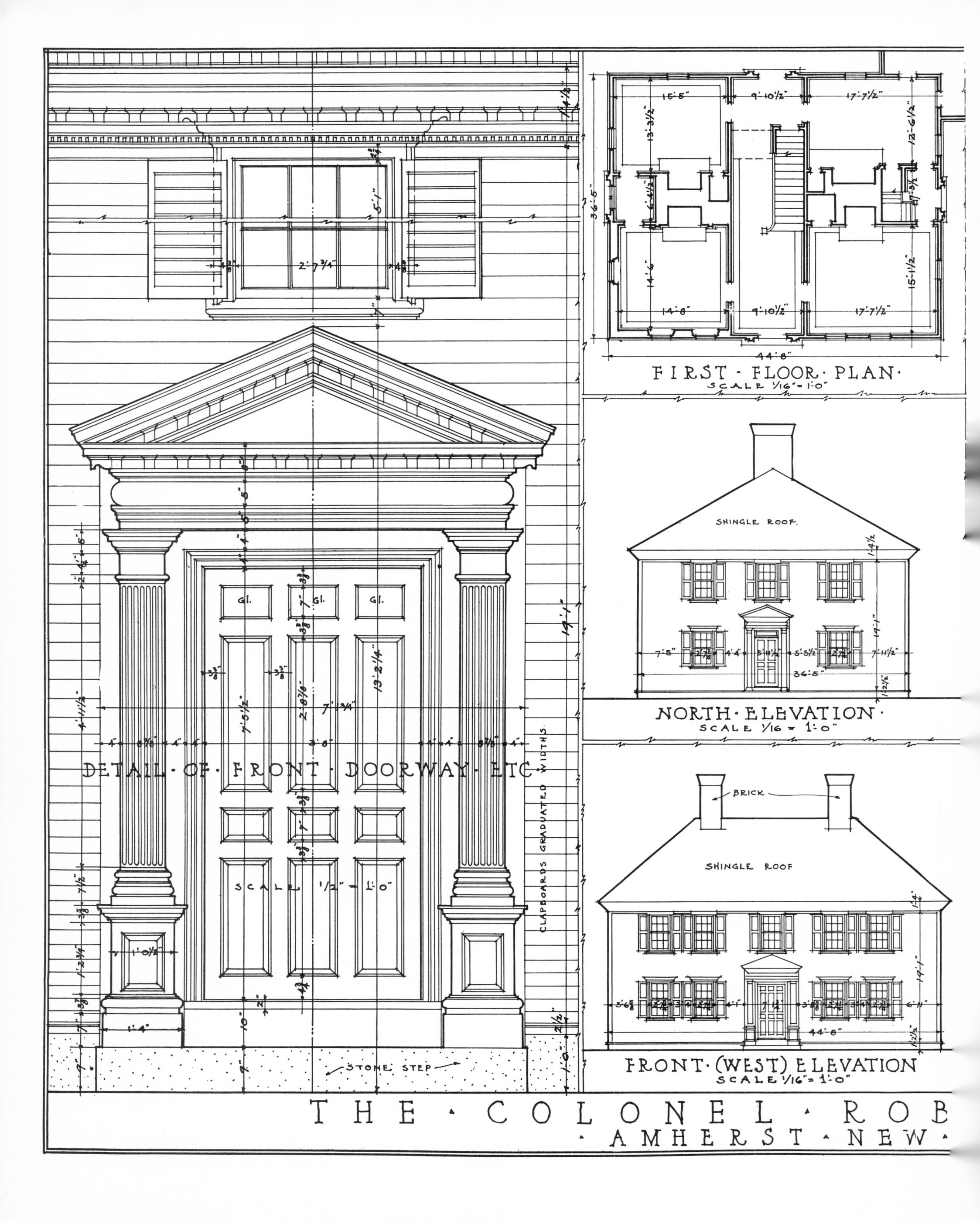
FIRST · FLOOR · PLAN ·
SCALE 1/16" = 1'-0"
SHINGLE ROOF
NORTH · ELEVATION ·
SCALE 1/16 = 1'-0"
BRICK
SHINGLE ROOF
FRONT · (WEST) ELEVATION
SCALE 1/16" = 1'-0"
DETAIL · OF · FRONT · DOORWAY · ETC
SCALE 1/2" = 1'-0"
CLAPBOARDS GRADUATED WIDTHS
STONE STEP
THE · COLONEL · ROB
· AMHERST · NEW ·

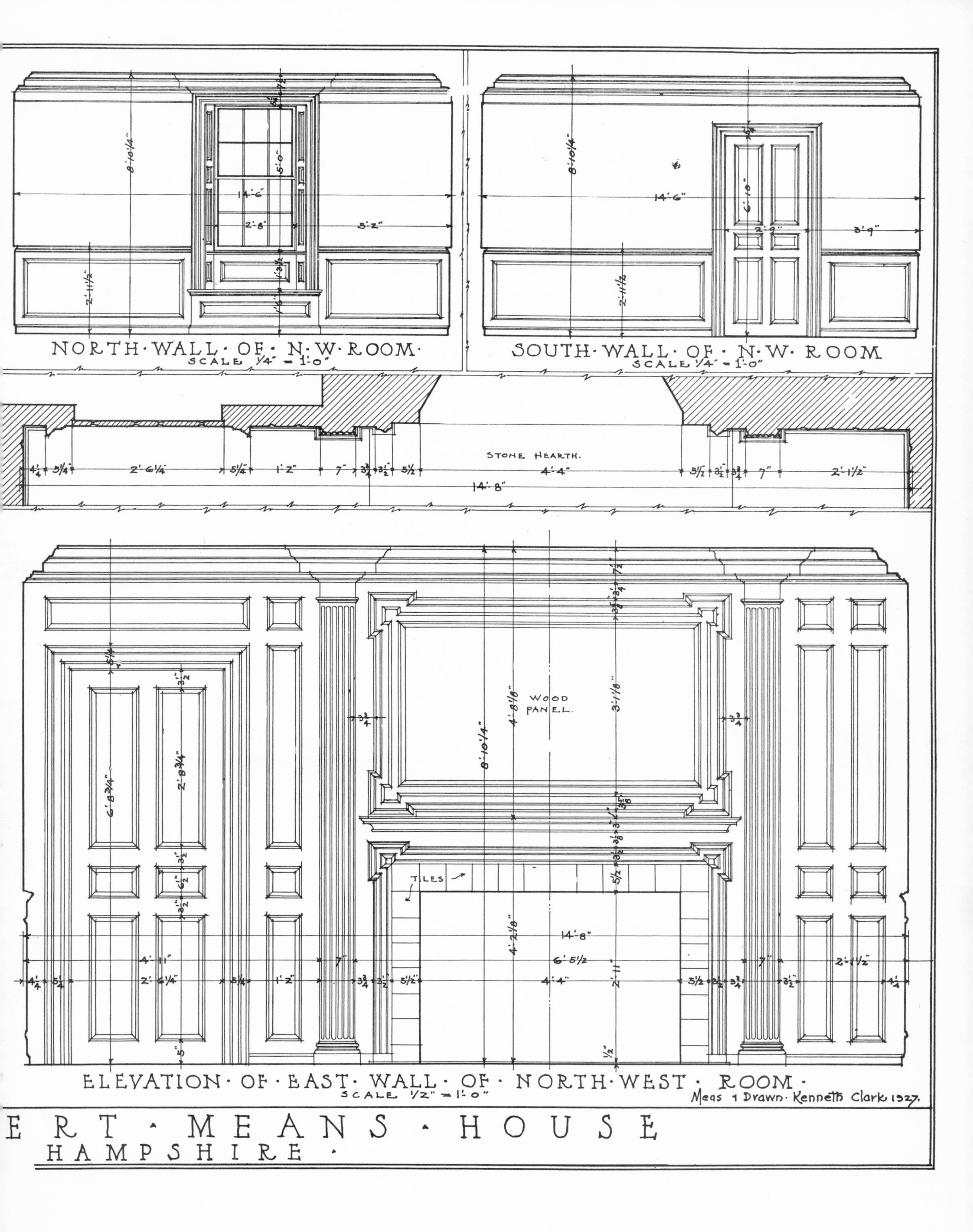
NORTH · WALL · OF · N · W · ROOM ·
SCALE 1/4" = 1'-0"
SOUTH · WALL · OF · N · W · ROOM
SCALE 1/4" = 1'-0"
STONE HEARTH.
WOOD PANEL.
TILES
ELEVATION · OF · EAST · WALL · OF · NORTH · WEST · ROOM ·
SCALE 1/2" = 1'-0"
Meas + Drawn · Kenneth Clark 1927.
ERT · MEANS · HOUSE
HAMPSHIRE ·

THE ORIGINAL KITCHEN—NOW USED AS A DINING ROOM

THE BACK STAIRCASE

THE SOUTH DOORWAY

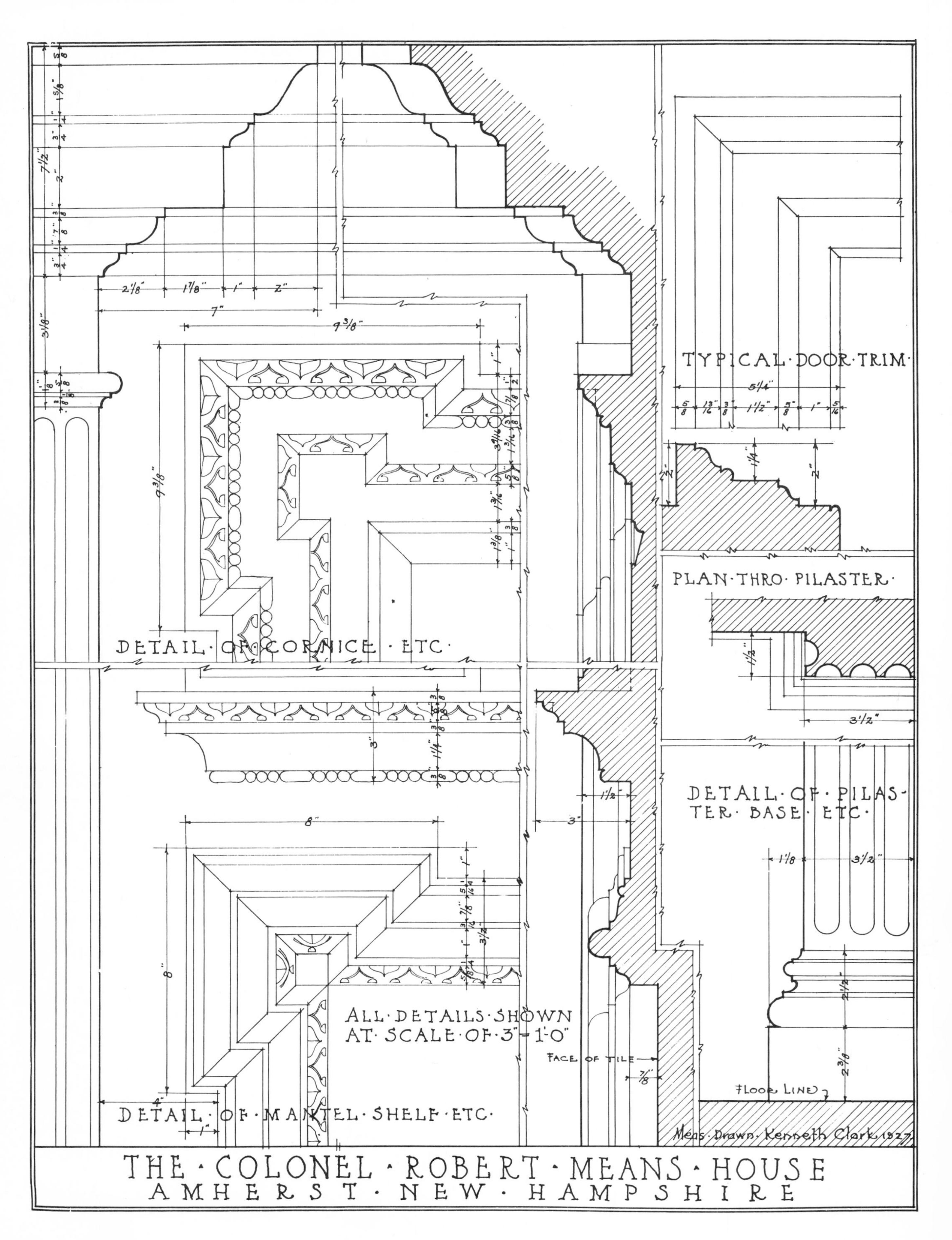
TYPICAL·DOOR·TRIM·
PLAN·THRO·PILASTER·
DETAIL·OF·CORNICE·ETC·
DETAIL·OF·PILASTER·BASE·ETC·
ALL·DETAILS·SHOWN AT·SCALE·OF·3"=1'-0"
FACE OF TILE
FLOOR LINE
DETAIL·OF·MANTEL·SHELF·ETC·
Meas·Drawn·Kenneth Clark 1927
THE·COLONEL·ROBERT·MEANS·HOUSE
AMHERST·NEW·HAMPSHIRE

DETAIL OF MANTEL IN THE PARLOR

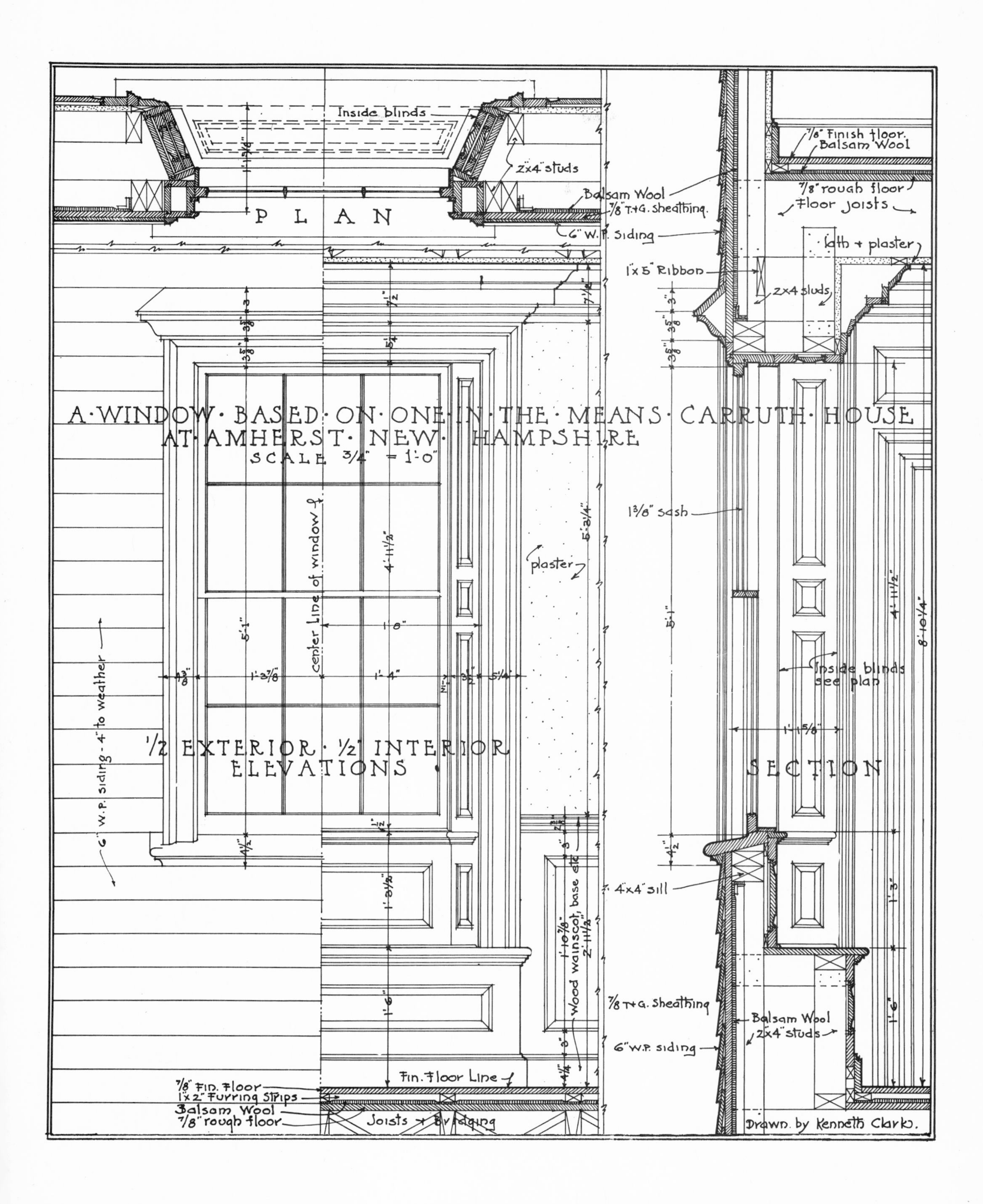
PLAN
Inside blinds
2x4" studs
Balsam Wool
7/8" T+G. sheathing.
6" W.P. siding
7/8" Finish floor.
Balsam Wool
7/8" rough floor
Floor joists
lath + plaster
1x5" Ribbon
2x4 studs
A·WINDOW·BASED·ON·ONE·IN·THE·MEANS·CARRUTH·HOUSE
AT·AMHERST·NEW·HAMPSHIRE
SCALE 3/4" = 1'-0"
1 3/8" sash
center Line of window
plaster
Inside blinds see plan
6" W.P. siding - 4" to weather
1/2 EXTERIOR · 1/2 INTERIOR ELEVATIONS
SECTION
4"x4" sill
Wood wainscot, base etc
7/8 T+G. Sheathing
Balsam Wool
2x4" studs
6" W.P. siding
Fin. Floor Line
7/8" Fin. Floor
1x2" Furring Strips
Balsam Wool
7/8" rough floor
Joists + Bridging
Drawn by Kenneth Clark.

View from South-West, (1936) on Original Site
THE COL. PAUL WENTWORTH MANSION—1701—SALMON FALLS, NEW HAMPSHIRE

# Colonel Paul Wentworth Mansion

THE Wentworth Mansion at Salmon Falls was built by a grandson of Elder William Wentworth, born in England in 1617, who came to this country in 1639 to found an American branch of an old and famous English family. Many of his descendants still reside in and about Portsmouth, N. H. The dwelling built by the Elder's oldest son, Samuel, probably about 1670, just "south of Liberty Ridge and Puddle Dock," was in existence up to about 1926, and its principal room and staircase are now incorporated in the American Wing of the Metropolitan Museum, in New York.

The fourth son of Elder William was Ezekiel (born 1651) who had six children. Ezekiel's second son (born in 1678) was Paul, and his third son was Benjamin, whose son, John, inherited the Salmon Falls property from his Uncle, by a will made in 1747-48. Paul was a first cousin of Governor Benning Wentworth (born 1696) whose father had been brought up with his on Garrison Hill, nearby, in Dover, N. H. Paul's father, Ezekiel, had settled at Salmon Falls, and it was therefore easy for his son, Paul, to establish himself on the top of a commanding knoll, nearby the falls named from the salmon that came up the river. There he established a sawmill, and conducted a profitable business in supplying lumber for the rapidly growing and important town of Portsmouth, at the river's mouth, and for export to England.

Long before 1936, the water power at Salmon Falls had caused the town to develop into a manufacturing community; the railroad had been carried directly in front of the old house; and it was no longer a suitable or pleasant site for the later generations of the family, who still owned the old mansion. In order to preserve the structure and continue it in use, therefore, it was taken down in the fall of 1936, piece by piece, and transported to an appropriately rural—if quite different—site, beside another river, in Dover, Massachusetts, where it could become the home of new generations. And in the process of taking the old dwelling apart, many details of its past use and history were disclosed, to the recording of which this present publication is to be principally restricted.

First it should be said that as the house stood in Salmon Falls it contained no recent or "modern" improvements. No plumbing or heating had ever been added. It had been occupied of late years only in summer, and kept practically as a Residential Museum; the family, when in residence, having meals in the old barn nearby, which had been equipped with more modern cooking conveniences. And the house, when removed, has been as carefully maintained in all its original rooms, with no change, other than to introduce some inconspicuous electric and heating outlets. A small, but conveniently modern, kitchen has been installed, with a Maid's room over, in an eighteen foot extension of the old "Beverly Ell" to the East. The old fireplace in the "lean-to kitchen" has been restored, and the kitchen made, by inconspicuous minor changes, into the actual living room of the house. The lean-to was widened by three feet, to obtain necessary room, so that all modern plumbing, closets, etc., could be contained within the old "dark Attic" in the lean-to over the kitchen. As all the paneling in the various rooms had been in-

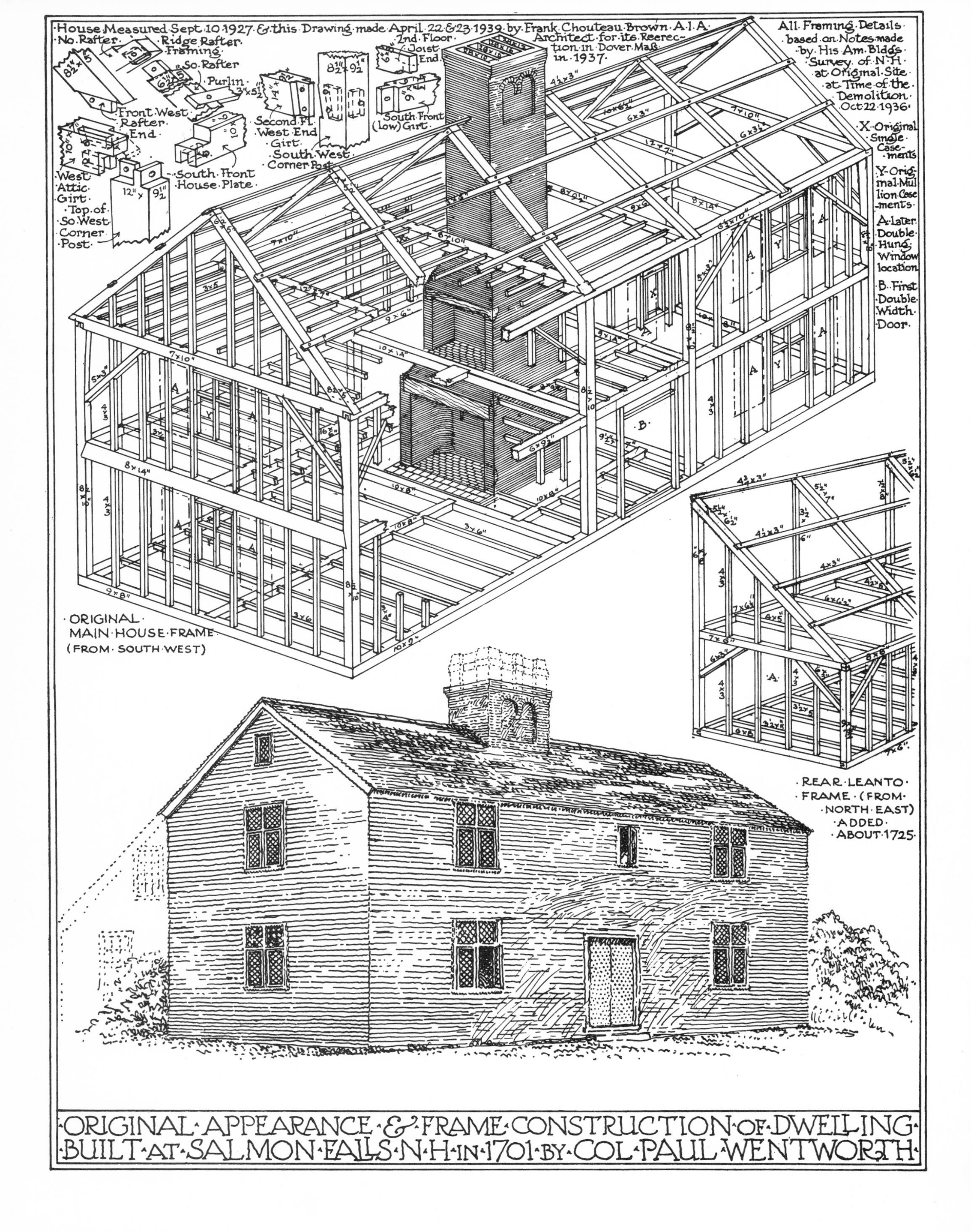
·House·Measured·Sept·10·1927·&·this·Drawing·made·April·22·&·23·1939·by·Frank·Chouteau·Brown·A·I·A·Architect·for·its·Reerection·in·Dover·Mass·in·1937·
·No.Rafter·
·Ridge·Rafter·Framing·
·So.Rafter·
·Purlin·
·Front·West·Rafter·End·
·Second·Fl·West·End·Girt·
·South·West·Corner·Post·
·2nd·Floor·Joist·End·
·South·Front·(low)·Girt·
·West·Attic·Girt·
·Top·of·So·West·Corner·Post·
·South·Front·House·Plate·
All·Framing·Details·based·on·Notes·made·by·His·Am·Bldgs·Survey·of·N·H·at·Original·Site·at·Time·of·the·Demolition·Oct·22·1936·
·X··Original·Single·Casements
·Y·Original·Mullion·Casements·
A·Later·Double·Hung·Window·location
·B··First·Double·Width·Door·
·ORIGINAL·MAIN·HOUSE·FRAME·(FROM·SOUTH·WEST)
·REAR·LEANTO·FRAME·(FROM·NORTH·EAST)·ADDED·ABOUT·1725·
·ORIGINAL·APPEARANCE·&·FRAME·CONSTRUCTION·OF·DWELLING·
·BUILT·AT·SALMON·FALLS·N·H·IN·1701·BY·COL·PAUL·WENTWORTH·

THE COL. PAUL WENTWORTH MANSION—1701—SALMON FALLS, NEW HAMPSHIRE

stalled after smaller fireplaces had been built within the original large openings, it was impossible to restore the original fireplaces, except in the "lean-to" kitchen-living room. The old fireplace originally in the dining room, was uncovered, however, and installed at Dover, Mass., in the new basement room immediately below the old dining room.

The original house was built as a four-room dwelling, with the usual central chimney and staircase against its south face, with casement windows, and a double width entrance doorway. Upon the rear, facing north, there were only three small, single casements and a kitchen door, which (according to the old accounts) connected through a low shed-like structure with the barn, at the northeast of the dwelling. The space along the low shed attic was the "slaves quarters."

LOOKING ACROSS VESTIBULE INTO PINE ROOM AT WEST (DOVER)
THE COL. PAUL WENTWORTH MANSION—1701—SALMON FALLS, NEW HAMPSHIRE

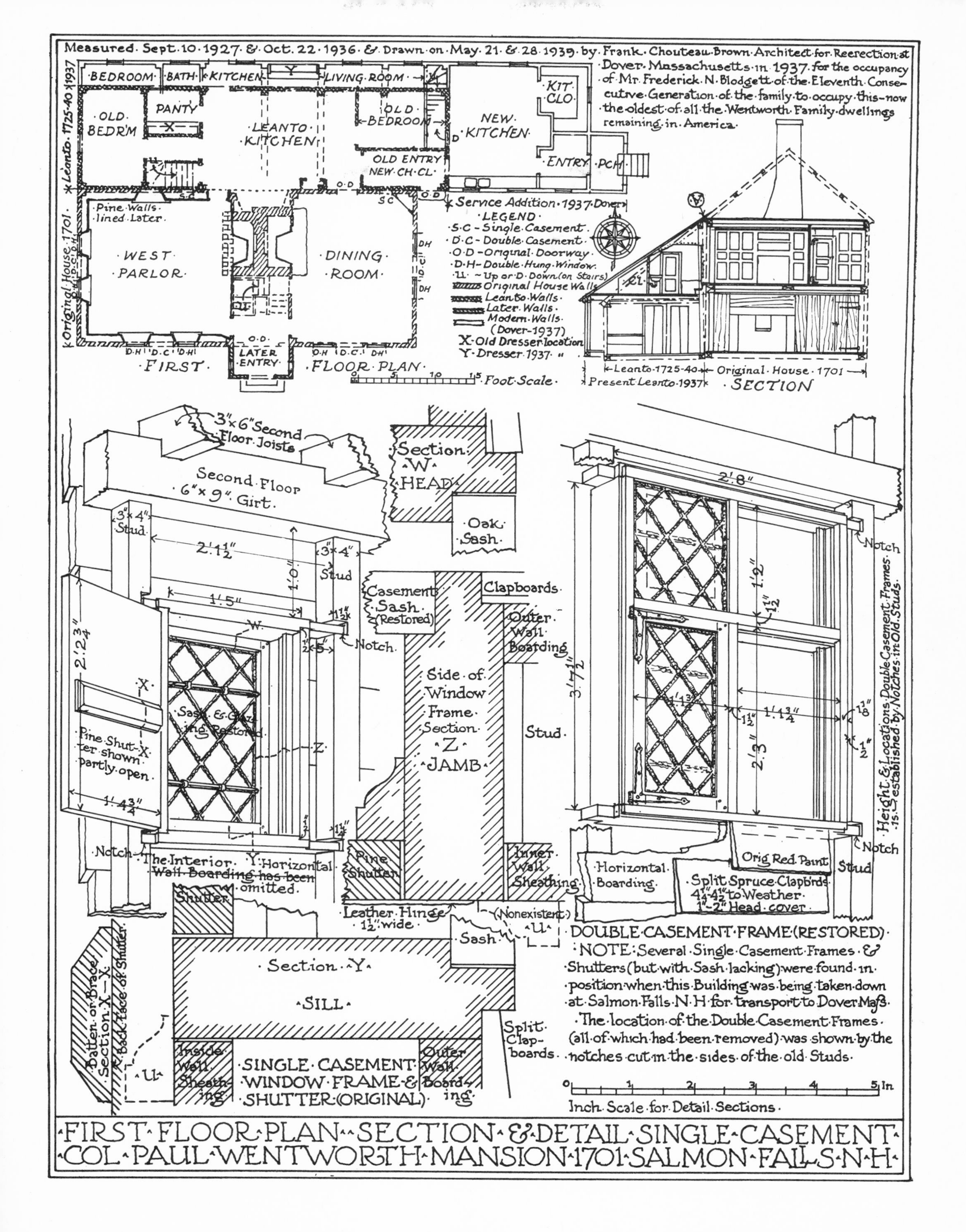
Measured Sept. 10 1927 & Oct. 22 1936 & Drawn on May 21 & 28 1939 by Frank Chouteau Brown Architect for Reerection at Dover Massachusetts in 1937 for the occupancy of Mr. Frederick N. Blodgett of the Eleventh Consecutive Generation of the family to occupy this—now the oldest of all the Wentworth Family dwellings remaining in America.
LEGEND
S.C – Single Casement
D.C – Double Casement
O.D – Original Doorway
D.H – Double Hung Window
U – Up or D – Down (on Stairs)
Original House Walls
Leanto Walls
Later Walls
Modern Walls (Dover-1937)
X – Old Dresser location
Y – Dresser 1937
FIRST FLOOR PLAN
Foot Scale
SECTION
Leanto 1725-40
Original House 1701
Present Leanto 1937
Service Addition 1937 Dover
WEST PARLOR
DINING ROOM
LEANTO KITCHEN
OLD BEDR'M
PANTY
OLD BEDROOM
NEW KITCHEN
OLD ENTRY NEW CH. CL.
LATER ENTRY
3"x6" Second Floor Joists
Second Floor 6"x9" Girt.
Section W HEAD
Oak Sash
Casement Sash (Restored)
Clapboards
Outer Wall Boarding
Side of Window Frame Section Z JAMB
Stud
Pine Shutter shown partly open
Sash & Glazing Restored
Notch
The Interior Horizontal Wall Boarding has been omitted.
Pine Shutter
Inner Wall Sheathing
Leather Hinge 1½" wide
(Nonexistent)
Section Y SILL
Inside Wall Sheathing
Outer Wall Boarding
Split Clapboards
Batten or Brace Section X–X
Back Face of Shutter
SINGLE CASEMENT WINDOW FRAME & SHUTTER (ORIGINAL)
Horizontal Boarding
Orig Red Paint
Split Spruce Clapbrds 4¼"-4½" to Weather 1"-2" Head cover
Height & Locations Double Casement Frames is established by Notches in Old Studs.
DOUBLE CASEMENT FRAME (RESTORED)
NOTE: Several Single Casement Frames & Shutters (but with Sash lacking) were found in position when this Building was being taken down at Salmon Falls N.H for transport to Dover Mass.
The location of the Double Casement Frames (all of which had been removed) was shown by the notches cut in the sides of the old Studs.
Inch Scale for Detail Sections
FIRST FLOOR PLAN SECTION & DETAIL SINGLE CASEMENT
COL PAUL WENTWORTH MANSION 1701 SALMON FALLS N.H

THE COL. PAUL WENTWORTH MANSION—1701—NOW AT DOVER, MASSACHUSETTS

THE COL. PAUL WENTWORTH MANSION—1701—SALMON FALLS, NEW HAMPSHIRE

THE COL. PAUL WENTWORTH MANSION—1701—SALMON FALLS, NEW HAMPSHIRE

The later lean-to, added sometime between 1725 and 1740— is unusual in the fact that it had a frame separate from the main house, where a space of about seven inches at the point marked "V," between the two frames.

While none of the double-casement frames was found in position, there could be no doubt as to their location and dimensions, as the notches into which these window frames fitted were disclosed in the original wall studding. Contrary to the usual belief, that double-hung windows were added at the original window locations, which were widened and lowered for that purpose, the frame structure and the floor plan show that the larger casements were centered in the rooms, and when the double-hung frames were added, they were placed *out*side the studs that had been set each side of the original double casements. This fact explains the somewhat closer spacing of the pairs of double-hung windows; and may be the reason for the similarly closer spacing that occurs on many another old house, as well!

An unusual contribution to our knowledge of old

OLD LEAN-TO, OR "DARK ATTIC," LOOKING EAST

PANELED CHAMBER, LOOKING TOWARD ORIGINAL FIREPLACE

THE COL. PAUL WENTWORTH MANSION—1701—SALMON FALLS, NEW HAMPSHIRE

East Family Chamber

looking toward Fireplace Side (Dover, 1939)

THE COL. PAUL WENTWORTH MANSION—1701—SALMON FALLS, NEW HAMPSHIRE

Detail of North-West Corner in Pine Parlor

Detail of Double faced Partition in Pine Chamber

THE COL. PAUL WENTWORTH MANSION—1701—SALMON FALLS, NEW HAMPSHIRE

Old Lean-to Kitchen with Original Fireplace (Restored) looking South-West
THE COL. PAUL WENTWORTH MANSION—1701—NOW AT DOVER, MASSACHUSETTS

building customs was made by the several single casement frames, which were found in place in the walls, covered by later paneling or changes, with their interior wooden shutters. These windows, along with some old split spruce clapboards, which still showed the old red paint, and rear eaves trim had been preserved under the lean-to. The one in the second story closet-room, back of the chimney, was easily seen in the attic in Salmon Falls. Unfortunately, none of these windows had retained either the sash or the leading; which have been supplied from contemporaneous material, along with the restoration of the double-casement window, developed to fit the spaces and notches found in the old house frame. The upper opening is shown with a fixed leaded filling, though a sash, if installed (as seems unlikely) has been outlined by dotted lines.

Old Lean-to Kitchen looking West (Salmon Falls)

But meanwhile, the double-hung sash windows had been installed in the principal rooms, even before the lean-to was added, as clearly appeared in the arrangement of the pine paneling on the north walls of the two rooms west of the fireplace. The pine walls in the West Parlor were probably added at this same time; but the double-faced partition and paneling in the bedroom over was probably added at a still later date; as was also the vestibule built out at the front entrance, and the changed staircase of the first flight, with its pine balustered rail. The original rail and buttress were left in the runs to the attic floor.

The paneling in the two east rooms was also of later date, and the corner cupboard was the result of at least two further changes. The very early wall paper in the east second story bedroom, still displaying the tax stamp with the English crown, was moved (along with the section of plaster wall upon which it was pasted), in one panel, the only piece of original plaster preserved in the dwelling in its new location.

The lean-to Kitchen (shown above, as it last stood at Salmon Falls) was the only old room much altered by the necessary uses of the various intervening generations. Its old windows had full-length sliding shutters, and beneath its floor was a shallow circular pit—or "Indian Cellar"—with original movable steps from the trap-door in the floor above. The original Kitchen fireplace has been rebuilt in Dover, with the old bricks, and the one from the West Parlor is restored in a room with primitive furniture and fittings beneath the present Dining Room. The Kitchen Dresser was found in the pantry and replaced in the Kitchen-Living Room.

View from River Bank (from North-West)
New Kitchen End and Garage at left
PAUL WENTWORTH MANSION, DOVER, MASS.

THE JEWETT HOUSE, SOUTH BERWICK, MAINE.

A remarkably well proportioned and delicate Roman Doric porch. Note the filling of the flutes in the lower third of the columns to avoid too great apparent slenderness in the columns.

# Houses of the Maine Coast

THE Yankee skipper feeling his way in the soft fog that lies along the southern Maine coast in August, watching the chart spread in the wheelhouse beside him, sees upon it the lines of the streams flowing southerly into the sea, as the rain drops run down a window-pane at the beginning of a shower. They waver in their courses as they swerve around highlands, now reaching straight through meadows and spreading into inland ponds, now tortuously winding amidst rocky ledges, but always tending southeasterly until they form estuaries up which the sea tide rushes to meet the waters from the forests and the hills.

Down these streams float the rafts of lumber from the pinelands, cut in the forests of Aroostook, and at the headwaters of the Androscoggin, the Penobscot, and the Kennebec. Deep in the forests, far up on the mountain side, lie the camps, busy through the white winters with the work of many lumbermen who are felling the monarchs of the trees, the tall, slender, straight white pines of the northland.

It is a strange anomaly that the white pine, with its home in a land of harsh winters, growing amidst the constant stress of wind and storm, should have a fiber straight as a ruled line, a surface soft and smooth as silk, and that its grain, instead of being gnarled and twisted, should be so even and fine that it will respond to the most delicate of carving.

The logs, brought down over the snows to the streams, float down in broad rafts to the more open reaches of the rivers, to the mill ponds where the streams are dammed, and there are sawn in lengths and widths, into scantling and plank and board, and sent to their destinations.

The Yankee skipper knows all of this. He has loaded his decks at the head of navigation and is now distributing his cargo. He knows every inch of the varied coast of Maine, the long fingers of land stretching out into the sea, the inlets, and bays, and islands, and reefs; and even in the fog he has little need of his chart, but the chart itself shows penetrating arms of the sea running deep into the land to meet the rivers, each of which ramifies into little bays and coves and back waters and into numerous almost landlocked harbors in which navies might ride. And, like the Greeks of Leigh Hunt, the skipper "is always putting up harbors and creeks," for there lie his markets which he can supply from the source directly.

The coast cities of Maine lie up these inlets, and in the cities and upon the banks of the bays and coves the merchants of Maine built their houses.

THE SEWELL HOUSE, YORK, MAINE.

Finely proportioned façade, simple fence with delicate urns, the square balusters to the fence are set diagonally to obtain the play of light and shade.

The first century after the Revolutionary War was one of active shipping interest in New England. The East India trade created a long and famous list of clipper ships, which gave prosperity not only to Salem, Newburyport and Portsmouth, but to Portland and Bath and other Maine coast towns.

The whaling fleets of Martha's Vineyard, Nantucket and New Bedford were aided by the Maine shipyards, and both commerce and shipbuilding industry brought prosperity.

In the years between the end of the Revolutionary War and the War of 1812 there is increasing evidence of comfortable fortunes having been amassed by local merchants all along the Atlantic coast, for larger and more important private houses are being built everywhere, not only in the towns themselves, but often at quite a distance from them. Especially is this the case in the first decade of the nineteenth century.

Sheltered from the sea by outlying islands, as at North Haven, or nestled in behind promontories or headlands, with still waters at the foot of grassy slopes, are to be found the homes of these amphibiously minded merchants of Maine, men who sent out their own ships and often commanded them and sailed from and came home to their own doors.

There are no more numerous or better landlocked harbors for "fitting out," while safely protected from all interference, than on the coast of Maine. The Dalmatian coast of the Adriatic and the gulfs of the Grecian peninsula alone compare with it. The famous *Bonne Homme Richard* of John Paul Jones was "fitted out" in the Great Bay up the Piscataqua River, and many a cargo has been laden from some concealed nook between York and Campobello.

Our Yankee skipper has been standing in closer to land, and suddenly he runs out of the fog into clear sunshine. As he emerges the long white mass of mist stretches right and left like a sheer wall cut by a knife. It seems as if by looking back he might see in it the hole he had left in emerging. The land breeze, dry and hot, is beating the fog out to sea, and before him is spread the charming fantastic coast of Maine: rocky ledges, gray at their crowns and russet and red and purple as they dip into the tide, upon their tops and sides twisted cedars and hardy savins, long reaches of green salt marsh, deeper touches of upland meadow, and every-

THE HOBBS HOUSE, SOUTH BERWICK, MAINE.
A very simple house of unusually good proportions.

THE JUDGE HAYES HOUSE, SOUTH BERWICK, MAINE.
Gabled type, ample in effect. Balustrade over porch unnecessary, too high.

where little or large inlets setting into the land.

Over the crest of one of these rocky hillocks are broad masses of spreading elms, grouped together as if planted with a purpose. That purpose is manifest as the point of land is weathered and the inlet opens, for amidst the trees is a broad white mass, a simple rectangular shape, set four-square to the winds, with a low-pitched roof and ample chimneys above it at each end. It is nestled among the trees, which were planted to give it shade from the summer's sun, and is the homestead of some merchant of Maine, or at least was such in the early days of the last century, and may at the present time be the summer home of a resident from a distant city.

It corresponds in a way with the planters' homes of Virginia, though it has no dependencies of the slave quarters, nor buildings for the housing of farm laborers. For the farm laborer of the North has usually a little home of his own at a distance. Also the income of this homestead

HOUSE AT WELLS, MAINE.
Well-proportioned façade, with wall texture refined by narrow clapboards.

THE ROBERT LORD HOUSE, KENNEBUNK, MAINE.
Type simulating stone upon façade by the use of matched sidings.

is not necessarily from the farm; it comes from merchant shipping, so that very often the farm buildings seem disproportionately small for the apparent importance of the house with which they are associated. But there may be a long L of outbuildings, or a considerable barn.

Many of the houses in Maine were built between 1800 and 1810. That decade is an important one in residential building in American Eastern cities. The early economies of the years following the Revolutionary War were no longer felt necessary, and comfortable living, such as had been in the Colonies before the great struggle, began to reappear.

The traditions of Colonial architecture had not been disturbed by the turgid stream from other sources that later appeared. When relations were reëstablished with England, importations of the minor factors of house building again made their appearance. Hardware, wall papers, relief ornaments for mantels, etc., were often brought from London, but a skilled race of New England carpenters and of carvers had been created who, however, manifestly looked to the English pattern books, published and republished since 1700, for their designs of mouldings, cornices, and entablatures, for portals, and even for façades, which latter fact somewhat accounts

THE ROBERT LORD HOUSE,
KENNEBUNK, MAINE.

THE SMITH HOUSE, WISCASSET, MAINE.

Admirable cornices, both upon main façade and the smaller masses. Note the angle of these cornices is more acute than 45 degrees, which is usually the case in Colonial exteriors, and gives an effect of additional refinement.

for the custom of often confining the architectural treatment to the façade alone, leaving the other elevations largely to take care of themselves, and also for the different surface treatment of façades to imitate stone antecedents, while the ends were frankly clapboarded or at times built of brick.

The classic styles originated in wood, the columns were tree-trunks, the facias boards, the mouldings cleats; and the reversion to wood in America was the most natural thing in the world. The style was going back to its original ancestry and in doing so became delicate and refined. For there is nothing so manifestly absurd as an excessive use of bulk of wood, both for æsthetic and structural reasons. The classic wooden architecture of New England gives evidence of a very intelligent use of the material, which was maintained after the Georgian style in England became heavy and dull and cumbrous. That this is largely due to an appreciation of the possibilities of wood, and of white pine especially, is constantly manifest. Seldom in these houses of the early nineteenth century is there excess of material, their charm being that of simplicity without crudeness, based upon proportions obtained from the books of English masters.

The work in New England, somewhat more indigenous than elsewhere in the States, was more refined in its detail than elsewhere. There is more attention paid to entasis of columns, to fineness of fillets, to subtlety of curved profiles to mouldings. The fact is interesting, for English detail was less careful in contrasting sections, and in delicacy and avoidance of monotony. A comparison of Virginian Colonial details which were derived at a better period directly from England justifies this statement.

It is known that many of the New England carpenters were also ship carpenters and figure-head carvers, and there is no education relating to the beauty of lines and curves better than that obtained in designing ships. An appreciation of line and form became second nature to these men, and when it was associated with so admirable and amenable a material as white pine, it would be strange if the results were not good.

Necessary economies also created the restraint so essential in fine classic architecture. An interesting example of this is shown by the illustrations of two houses in Wiscasset. One, the William Nickels house, was built in 1807–08, and has both upon piazza and the house itself a very admirable Corinthian order without modillions but with double rows of contrasting dentils, Greek in feeling. The piazza balustrade was unfortunately added about 1890 with no regard for or knowledge of the charm of the old work. Mr. Abiel Wood began his house in 1812 with the distinct intention of outdoing the Nickels house, but had to practise economy, and, taking several years to complete the house, omitted the pilaster treatment; yet the house is bettered in its proportions, especially in those of the Palladian windows in the second story, and the arched window over it in the third story. This latter window is a favorite terminal factor of the axis motive of a façade in houses on the Maine coast, though not peculiar to them.

The question of proportions is always somewhat intangible and often houses with the least embellishment give an impression of the greater

THE SMITH HOUSE, WISCASSET, MAINE.

Extremely well proportioned, having almost monumental quality. There is a good portal behind the storm porch.

THE ABIEL WOOD HOUSE, WISCASSET, MAINE.
Simple and well proportioned.

distinction. Classic architecture originates as a one-storied style, it progresses as a two-storied style, and later still more stories are added. The difficulty of adding these stories successfully increases geometrically with the increasing number of stories. This must necessarily be the case, as with the addition of each story the design departs farther from the original source of its inspiration. Therefore some of the smaller and simpler two-storied houses of more modest type built outside the towns are sometimes the more attractive.

It was to such houses as these that the coaster brought her lumber, landing it on the shore below the site, where the frame was cut and mortised and tenoned and pinned, with the strong corner posts which so often show in the rooms and become cased pilasters. It was here that, after each side had been put together upon the ground, the day of the house-raising was observed, bringing together the interested neighbors and celebrated by a liberal distribution of hard cider to the workmen. And later the coasters bring the boards and sidings and clapboards, and the stock of greater thickness for the pilasters, all of which is planed and fitted to as near perfection as the carpenter, proud of his reputation for skill, can perform his work. The fluted columns, the dentil courses with the infinite variations, which characterize so much of this work, were probably done in a neighboring town, of the finest, clearest white pine, without a blemish, thoroughly dried, and a pleasure to look upon even before it was touched by a plane. The carving may have come from farther afield. Pieces of English carving in mahogany made by some London master, even perhaps by Grinling Gibbons himself, have been found behind the paint of New England mantels, having been imported and used as models and repeated in the remainder of the work in white pine.

Two of the simpler two-storied buildings are illustrated: one the Hobbs house at South Berwick, the other at Wells, not many miles away; one on the river, the other not far from the shore. The Hobbs house could not be simpler, but its proportions are admirable, and the details refined. Its hopper roof is surmounted by a balustrade of plain cylindrical balusters, well spaced.

In studying the books from which the carpenters worked, it will be noticed that they are lacking in examples of good turnings, and the weakest details of many otherwise excellent Colonial designs are in the balusters. This is not the case with staircase balusters. The Hobbs house balustrade and the fence to the Sewell house at York, indicate that turnings are not necessary, and that they may be too small in scale for the rest of the work.

The smaller houses seldom are covered with the broad matched sidings which were used to give the appearance of the smooth surface of a stone ashlar face. This work was confined to the more ambitious examples and upon their main façades. But the clapboards which covered most of the walls were not of the coarse modern variety, laid as per specification 4¼ inches to the weather. On the contrary, they were clear and thin and often laid three inches to the weather, and at times the widths of the overlaps were graded up the wall. The fine narrow spaces between the shadow lines gave scale and texture to the wall surface. These narrow clapboards are to be seen upon the Wells and York houses.

The Smith house at Wiscasset has a broad overlapping siding. This house is unusually fine in its proportions. Its end walls are brick, the thickness of the wall, painted white, showing at the ends of the façade. The cornices are fine in their thin overshooting angle, but the Ionic cap is heavy in its scrolls. The balustrade is very well proportioned to the mass of the house. The Sewell house at York has great distinction in proportions and an unusually fine portal with Ionic columns in antis. The broad simplicity of the details of the house and its vigor of treatment are exceptional. It has the dignity of late Georgian work with the finesse of the Colonial.

In the towns themselves, as in Salem and Newburyport and Portsmouth, the old sea captains and merchants built their houses almost directly upon the streets, the gardens at the back. These houses are treated usually with pilasters, either Ionic or Corinthian, running through two stories. If the house has three stories the lower story is made, as in the old Dole house in Portland and the Nickels house at Wiscasset, a high base or podium for the upper stories, not, as often occurs elsewhere, with the pilaster in the first two stories, and the third story an attic above the entablature. The outer pilasters are kept well in from the corner, thus announcing the fact that the architectural treatment is for ornament only. Also the entablature breaks thoroughly, the break being carried through the cyma, not stopping at the soffit of the facia, or planceer. The definition of stories by a belt course is usual, but not universal.

On the old Dole house the very delicate porch is surmounted by a villainous balustrade.

It will be noted in several of these houses that the center axis is accented by a third-story arched window, between the square openings at the sides. This is one of Palladio's novelties, of which he had several. It always looks interpolated, and is at its worst when the arch is doubled concentrically as in the Nickels house. It is a favorite motive in the first decade of the nineteenth century and an ill-advised one. A glance at the Sewell house at York will show that its omission is a virtue.

In the illustrations of portals, that of the Jewett house at South Berwick is unusually fine, and the treatment of fine herring-bone reeds in the pilasters of the Nickels house is unique and shows how effective can be a very simple method of obtaining interesting texture.

And so our skipper sails up the river, anchors off a pier, goes ashore in his boat, and spends his afternoon in the counting-house of one of the ship-owners, who is also a builder of the dignified houses of Maine. He may have done so in the early part of the last century, he may do so to-day, for still are the forests being felled, still is the white pine being sawn and planed and chiseled and carved, still are the houses being built, and, by good fortune, following the good old styles of years ago.

THE SEWELL HOUSE, YORK, MAINE.

**Dignified portal with adequate arch moulding. Note that the pilasters as well as the columns have entases.**

CHESTNUT STREET, CAMDEN, MAINE.

# Penobscot Bay, Maine

DOWN EAST! How many people in these United States think at once of the rustic paraphernalia of our famous drama. But east of Boston rather than "north of Boston" lies territory rich in the history of our country. East again of the Kennebec, the traveler will find places that can still show him how the country became great, provided he turn thoughtful eyes upon them.

Three names of Maine towns on Penobscot Bay will have a familiar sound to very many ears—Camden, Belfast, Castine. It was to see for ourselves what these names were attached to that we sailed up the coast from Boston, and climbed onto the little pier under the Camden hills in very good time for the last of a remarkably fine sunrise. The rugged, barrier hills behind, the little harbor below, were a delight to the eye, but the gigantic tops of serried elms climbing away to right and left along the foreshore, the peeping white gables, and jutting massive chimneys, spoke so eloquently of old days and a long past that all doubts were gone, and we could concentrate on breakfast reassured and expectant.

Names have a very effective way of cutting through the layers of time to the little kernel of event that matters, and here are three names that hint at stories: Camden; there is a Camden-town in London to-day. Belfast; Irish linen, shipyards, and Orangemen. Castine; Mediterranean, Latin, French, certainly not Anglo-Saxon; and there we have stories well begun.

Penobscot Bay was early known as a splendid waterway, marvelously timbered and desirable, which lay so midway between French Acadia and English Virginia that no man could safely say that King James or King Louis was lord of the realm. Its waters were explored first in 1605. France established a trading-post in 1629, at Bagaduce, which later became Castine. This they counted as their western outpost, and claimed all to the east of the bay as French. Later they found the Penobscot River was the great winter highway from Quebec to the Atlantic, so that the English coveted Castine, at the mouth of the river, and at last closed this door to France.

The Council of Plymouth received title to all the western shores of the bay from James I, and from this original grant, through inheritance and deed, title passed to a group of heirs. These gentlemen had great difficulties with one David Dunbar, "Surveyor of the king's woods," who requisitioned the entire coast for trees to make masts for the English navy, and forcibly stopped all colonization. The upshot of the matter was that Waldo went to London for the grantees and the Waldo Patent was confirmed in 1731. It was in 1769 that the first settler was given pos-

THE SMALL HOUSE, BELFAST, MAINE.

The Stevens House.

The Tilden House (Built 1796).

TWO DOORWAYS AT BELFAST, MAINE.

THE PERKINS HOUSE, CASTINE, MAINE. Built 1769.

session here at Camden by the "Twenty Associates," as the company of heirs was called. The town had already been named after Lord Camden, Waldo's "friend at court" during the action for the grant. The place was a hamlet when the Revolution came, and the settlers must have been terribly isolated. Small British privateers, known as "Shaving Mills," swept the coast and raided Camden, sometimes with success but often the honors did not go to the king's men.

At this time Belfast also had been settled, not like Camden, by individuals sent out by a company, but by a group of people whose fathers fifty years before, in 1718, had fled from North Ireland to Boston, settled Londonderry, N. H., and started the Irish potato in New England with poetic justice to become one of Maine's chief industries. A man, by name John Mitchell, came to the Belfast district, saw, and returned, to bring thirty-five of his friends, who promptly bought the site and petitioned for their ancestral name to be given it.

Castine, which now bears the name of a Count de Castine, a family since wiped out in France by the Revolution, was for a long time known as Bagaduce. The gentleman whose name it now bears was evidently an adventurous and enterprising soldier of fortune. As governor of what must have been a mere trading-post and fort, he at least left his name for the place, which was later abandoned by the French, and finally resettled by the English in 1761. The French name does not appear to have been used until after the Revolution. The fate of the Bagaduce expedition against this British fort may have led the townspeople to seek a name of better omen.

All this is to paint our picture of coast villages, kept from growing to towns first by the unpleasant relations of French and English and then by our own war for independence. So it was that most of our houses had to wait for their builders until the Revolution had been fought, and we can see what sort of towns the Yankees could, by sheer grit, bring into being during our lean and hungry "critical period" from 1790 to 1812. For these houses must have echoed to the rumors and alarms of the War of 1812.

These buildings are simple and the character of the times is written broadly across their almost gaunt faces. But, nevertheless, there is a real charm and an admirable character to such gauntness, especially when it is a characteristic developed on a face where inheritance and breeding are fine. That these builders were men of Massachusetts, with the background of Salem, Newburyport, Boston, Plymouth, and the settled stateliness of the Old Colony, there can be no doubt. It is interesting to see what they retained of their birthright, and what their modest means obliged them to forego.

In Camden the simpler types prevail and there is little rich detail. In Belfast a large number of Neo-Grec or Classic Revival houses complicate the situation. They give the town an air almost of opulence, and date its heyday thirty years later than Camden, in the time when whaling and lumber were beginning to make men's fortunes. All this work we have purposely omitted and stuck to the houses of earlier date. In Castine, both the fullness of detail and its very "colonial" character point both to an earlier date and a less limited financial condition. This town was the best known of the three during the days of the American sailing ships, and was the home of a fleet of merchant sailors who made every port from Liverpool to Bankok. "Castine" was painted under the stern of many a wind jammer known in the Indies and the China Seas.

Though our houses must have been nearly coeval, they divide into three general types: the one-story cottage, the two-story gabled farmhouse, and the square, hipped-roof mansion, with interior chimneys.

In Camden we have the three types all well represented. Of the cottage types only the doorways have been chosen for reproduction, but the pictures on give one a fair idea of the height of the façade, the ample wall, and widely spaced windows. The very considerable height from window head to cornice should be noted. This logical result of a good half-story under the roof is often slighted in our modern adaptations, to the detriment of the façade. All these cottages were originally built with a large central chimney, and a minute stairway, built between chimney and front door, in a tiny entrance hall.

The more well-to-do citizens, however, seem to have universally seized on the square plan, with two chimneys built into the cross wall dividing the front from the back rooms. The great depth of plan resulting from such a scheme necessitated the hip roof, and the pitch seems to have been flattened through economy even lower than the Massachusetts prototype. In every case the fenestration is excellent, the openings broad and ample, and the wall spaces kept even wider than the windows, commonly by grouping the side windows in pairs and thus gaining exterior wall surface even when the shutters were open. With no exceptions the windows were kept well away from the corners, and all the houses show a fine wide corner "pier" and have a resulting air of solidity.

With the possible exception of those in Castine, these houses all show decidedly the thrice removed influence of the illustrious Adam brothers. The universally over-delicate mouldings, the lack of projection of the cornices, the very delicate sash and window frames, the almost universal frontispiece door, in preference to a porch, point not so much to poverty as to the following of a model. The model is not hard to find in Massachusetts, where the Adam influ-

THE CARLETON HOUSE, CAMDEN, MAINE.

THE JOHNSON HOUSE, CASTINE, MAINE.

THE BENJAMIN FIELD HOUSE, BELFAST, MAINE.

THE STEVENS HOUSE, BELFAST, MAINE.

HOUSE ON CHESTNUT STREET, CAMDEN, MAINE.

ence came by way of the handbooks from England. These books are well known, and were the usual guides of the carpenter designers. The restraint of this work in Maine cannot be entirely ascribed to poverty, for the mouldings are good in profile, the doorways well designed, and the finish never stinted. It would have cost no more to coarsen all the detail, or to misplace the motives of the composition. They succeeded in achieving a grand manner in the most straightforward way. They stuck to good proportion, they used forms throughout which had been demonstrated successful for execution in wood, and they erred on the side of simplicity and thinness of details, both admirable faults in buildings built of wood. Clapboards were kept uniformly very narrow, and even the side and cross rails of the shutters were made narrow on the face, to keep in scale with the other detail: no attempt was made to use stone derived quoins, cornices, or pilasters, and the frontispiece doorways were so refined and attenuated as to lose their stone-cut character. These are as frankly wood built houses as could be asked for.

A few of the details are worth notice. The frontispiece doorways nearly all have the overhead fanlight in form of an arch either round or elliptical, sometimes glazed, sometimes filled with a wooden slab fan. Is it not possible that the absence of porches is partly due to the extremely mild summers, and the dark winters, requiring maximum light in the stair hall entry? It is noticeable that the doors are frequently fitted with slat shutters, which again shows the desire for a modified ventilation in the breezy summer afternoons. It is a pity that so many of the present owners have painted their sash black or dark green. The loss of the sparkle of the brilliant muntins in the dark openings is a serious one. Screens and screen doors are accursed by photographers of architecture. Some one can make a fortune by the invention of an invisible screen door, but not too invisible.

Cornices of the general type shown in the photograph of the Johnson house in Castine are frequent and deserve respectful study for their wooden scale and richness combined with simplicity. Notice, too, in this picture the thoroughly workmanlike and pleasing way in which the brick end has been joined with the clapboarded front. It becomes frankly a brick end due to two enormous end chimneys, and not a brick house finished with wood, as sometimes appears when the thickness of the brick wall shows on the front. The little side porch of this house is mainly wood—no attempt here to ape stone forms. The cap is gotten out of one stick with the shaft, and the diminution and entasis result. The stable wing of the Adams house at Castine is certainly playful enough use of stone forms. This is good carpentry and composition.

Lack of space forbids the reproduction of the

COTTAGE ON MOUNTAIN STREET.

DOORWAY,
THE PERKINS HOUSE, CASTINE, MAINE.

little church on the green at Castine. It is a smaller scale variant of the Belfast church and the latter was probably built afterward, and is doubtless an echo. It is certainly more successful as far as the tower goes, and shows improvements in detail but lacks the charm of the little one-story structure, which, without galleries, can have a fine side-window motive.

The Perkins house at Castine must be placed in a paragraph by itself. It stands alone among our collection as a pre-Revolutionary example. The mass and the character are frankly English, foursquare, and solid. It is evident that the ell toward the road is an addition, in fact the patching of the clapboarding is visible in the photograph. Neither Asher Benjamin nor Batty Langley had anything to do with this house. The steep pitch of the roof, the heavy solid frames of the windows, moulded and doweled, projecting far outside the clapboards, the unevenly divided sash with twenty lights, the blunt cornice, nowhere show the Adam influence. In fact the date of the original house is 1769, and the addition can have been but little later. The vestibule porch is comparatively modern, but is well handled and adds materially to the general effect of the house.

The detail photograph of the doorway gives one also a fair idea of the window frames and sash, and the unusual location of the glass practically on the same plane as the clapboards. This detail also occurs in the oldest house in Camden, otherwise ruinously altered. It may be a stretch of the imagination, but in contrast to all our other doorways this seems to be much more obviously of stone origin. Its wide, flat faces and broad, well-curved mouldings and thick fillets are much more early Georgian than what we usually call Colonial. Perhaps the model came rather from Sir William Chambers than Robert Adam. Notice, too, the excessive entasis of the pilasters.

That no one ever reads an architectural article to the bitter end is a commonplace among architects, so perhaps we are safe in stepping out before the falling curtain and speaking an epilogue to the empty house. Let us be as old-fashioned as our houses, and point a moral.

In these days, when financial solons cry to the world, "Work and save," and the man in the street sees dollars grow as big as harvest moons, the simple house of wood is suddenly a thing of virtue, preaching economy by the roadside. These Penobscot houses, simple to baldness, built in similar stringent times, embody all the virtues we would like to practise: rigid economy, dignity, good taste, good proportion, refinement, honesty, and, in spite of austerity, charm. If any of our pictures or any of our words help toward these results in the plain houses of to-day, this article has not been amiss.

MISS SMART'S COTTAGE, CHESTNUT STREET

STABLE WING,
THE ADAMS HOUSE, CASTINE, MAINE.

THE AMES HOUSE, WISCASSET, MAINE

# Wiscasset, Maine

IT IS claimed that DeMonts and Champlain, French pioneers in the New World, in the course of their exploration of the Maine coast, in 1605, ascended the Sheepscot River to what is now Wiscasset, and, although impressed with the beauty and majesty of its shores and the ease of access from the sea, they, learning that George Waymouth, the Englishman, had but a few weeks earlier planted the cross of St. George at what is now known as St. George's River as a token of discovery and possession, returned not hither. At what date Englishmen came to live here is not known with certainty; but it does appear from a deed given by three Indian Sagamores of this river, in 1663, to George Davie, an English seaman, who is believed to have come hence from Cornwall or Devon, in England, that Davie was then a resident of the Sheepscot region. Here he continued until he and his family were driven away by Indians in the time of King Philip's War. He returned but was finally driven off with all the other white settlers here in the next Indian War. Under the deed mentioned, and subsequent deeds from the Sagamores named, and by his rights by improvement and possession Davie claimed lands situate on both sides of the river and including the site of Wiscasset. Such rights descended to his heirs, from whom they passed by sale to persons interested in re-settling the lands here, but the hardships of a frontier life retarded the growth of population following the beginning of such re-settlement in 1729, and corporate existence was not attained until 1760.

Gradually a considerable export trade developed, consisting principally of forest products, such as white pine, oak and other primeval growths,—a trade which was pursued with varying fortunes throughout the hardships of the Revolutionary War and the later spoliations by the French. The nineteenth century brought a remarkably prosperous expansion, the neutral position of our government with relation to the Napoleonic wars permitting cargoes to be carried into European ports under the United States flag, and it was facetiously said that Wiscasset milked the British cow. Although that period of roaring trade was short-lived, the wealth of the merchants and shipowners increased so greatly that it was soon reflected in all trades and professions and was signalized by the erection of the many fine mansions which are the distinguishing reminders of the briefly enduring fortunes of that time.

Conspicuous among such mansions is that which was built for Capt. William Nickels, a retired master mariner who had become largely interested in commerce and navigation, with resulting prosperity. Upon its site originally stood the first two-story house erected at Wiscasset Point. With increase of wealth, desiring greater luxury of living and expansion of his hospitality, he rolled the old house back to a lot but a few rods distant, where it now stands, and in 1807 and 1808 he caused a new house to be built. This house, with its lofty front and rich ornamentation of carving, has ever

THE COURT HOUSE, WISCASSET, MAINE

been an object of admiration, and passing tourists to-day stay their speed at sight of it. Tradition has it that two years'time was devoted to finishing its front hall; that the services of one man were required to keep its hearth fires of wood supplied through the winter seasons; that it was noted for its magnificent banquets and entertainments; and an inventory of its furnishings of that period reveals that this house was the abode of the cultured and wealthy. The more ancient Nickels manors, situate in Lincoln County, are still notable for their substantial and elaborate construction, but the mansion of William Nickels surpasses them all.

No less conspicuous in the time to which this writing relates were the houses of the Woods, headed by that of Gen. Abiel Wood, who began a long business life in Wiscasset as early as 1768 and whose title was derived from his connection with the Massachusetts militia. His three-story mansion, now demolished, stood near the shore and, although of earlier date than that of Captain Nickels, is said to have resembled it in size and wealth of detail. The construction of that of his son, Hon. Abiel Wood, a noted merchant, banker, ship-owner and politician, who at one time represented the Lincoln District in Congress, was begun during the War of 1812, for the momentum of Wiscasset commerce carried part way through that disastrous time; but business reverses compelled suspension of work upon it for several years, as well as the elimination of some of the original specifications, and occupancy by the owner was not enjoyed until October, 1824. The house stands in a commanding location at the terminus of High Street and it is now occupied by descendants of the original owner. The houses of his brothers, Joseph Tinkham Wood and Hartley Wood, have also been preserved. The Joseph Tinkham Wood house, dating from 1805, was subjected to alteration in 1858, but certain of its most interesting features were fortunately retained and it is still notable for its stately entrance and its beautiful front hall and winding staircase. Wood's occupancy of it was cut short when he traded the house, and the land where it stands, to Moses Carlton, Jr., for a cargo of rum then recently landed on the latter's wharf in Wiscasset and valued at $12,000; and from Carlton's occupancy of fifty years it is more commonly known as the Carlton house. The Hartley Wood house, of less pretentious construction but still noteworthy in certain details, is now the summer home of the talented actress, Claire Eames.

We have seen that Wiscasset was incorporated in 1760. Its original corporate name was Pownalborough, it being thus called in honor of Thomas Pownall, who was then Governor of the Province of Massachusetts Bay, the jurisdiction of which extended over what is now the State of Maine. At about the time of the incorporation of Pownalborough a new county was established in these "Eastern parts," and Pownalborough was made the shire town, the courts of which were at first, and for several years, held in the western precinct adjacent to the Kennebec River. The advantages of Wiscasset harbor exceed those of that section around the Kennebec, and they were so rapidly availed of after the Revolutionary War closed that the growth of business and population at Wiscasset Point led to the removal of the courts hither,—all unitedly attracting ambitious young men to locate here. The corporate name was soon afterward changed to Wiscasset.

And so came Silas Lee, a native of Concord, Massachusetts, who graduated at Harvard College in 1784. Establishing himself at Wiscasset, where he ever after resided, Lee's law practice increased apace. He also entered political life, and while a Member of the Congess he resigned his post to accept an appointment by President Jefferson as United States Attorney for the District of Maine.

Early in the period of his residence here, Lee began to acquire real estate, and eventually secured several very desirable parcels, a part of which he developed with apparent profit. Of such lands he at first selected for a place of residence that through which High and Lee streets now run, and the first house that he put up was that in High Street which is now known as the Smith house. It is suggested that this house dates from 1792 for, although an earlier date has been assigned for its erection, it was not until that year that Lee cleared off a cloud upon the title, arising under the claims of the Wiscasset Proprietors, to the land where it stands. It ranges on a line with the Abiel Wood house and the Carlton house on that side of High Street which, from an architectural point of view, has been called the most interesting in Maine. In his journal of travels in Maine in 1796 the Rev. Paul Coffin alluded to this house as "the noble edifice of Lawyer Lee." On the same tour he noticed that Wiscasset then had "eight or ten majestic houses, and many decent, and of a common two-story size."

Judge Lee sold his High Street house to Gen. David Payson in June, 1807. Shortly after the death of Gen. Payson, in 1831, the house passed into the hands of Samuel E. Smith, who at about that time was Governor of the State of Maine, and it is now the home of his

HOUSE OVERLOOKING THE HARBOR, WISCASSET, MAINE

descendants.

Judge Lee's manners and address were distinguished for suavity, and at their several houses he and Mrs. Lee were fond of entertaining the Justices of Supreme Judicial Court and other dignitaries and men of parts who visited Wiscasset, and pleasing traditions of their fragrant hospitality may yet be encountered.

Near by the Smith house, and at the head of The Common, stands the Lincoln County Courthouse, the oldest building in Maine in which courts are now held. Its beautiful façade is notable for the perfect arches of its front windows and door. The date of its erection is shown by the simple but charming figures, 1824, which appear on the small, marble keystone in the arch at the entrance. This is the only one of the buildings here mentioned the cost of which is known, such cost being shown in the accounts of the agent for its construction as $10,843.09. Since May, 1825, terms of the Supreme Judicial Court have been held in this courthouse. Terms of United States courts have been held here; and at the bar have appeared the celebrated Jeremiah Mason, then of Boston, and many other distinguished lawyers, including Daniel Webster, "then," as one of his associates afterwards wrote, "in the full flush of his success and in the zenith of his power as a master of eloquence."

Looking at the spruce frame of a building erected in Wiscasset in 1872, William Chick, of many years' experience in house building, remarked: "Well, spruce is good lumber, but white pine is good enough for me." It was he who kept for many years a few well seasoned white-pine planks so that when his end should come, good white-pine lumber would be available for a water-tight box to hold his coffin.

STAIRWAY DETAIL

THE LEE-SMITH HOUSE, WISCASSET, MAINE [BUILT ABOUT 1792]
*Now known as the Governor S. E. Smith House*

# *The* LEE-SMITH HOUSE WISCASSET, MAINE

MEASURED DRAWINGS *from*
*The George F. Lindsay Collection*

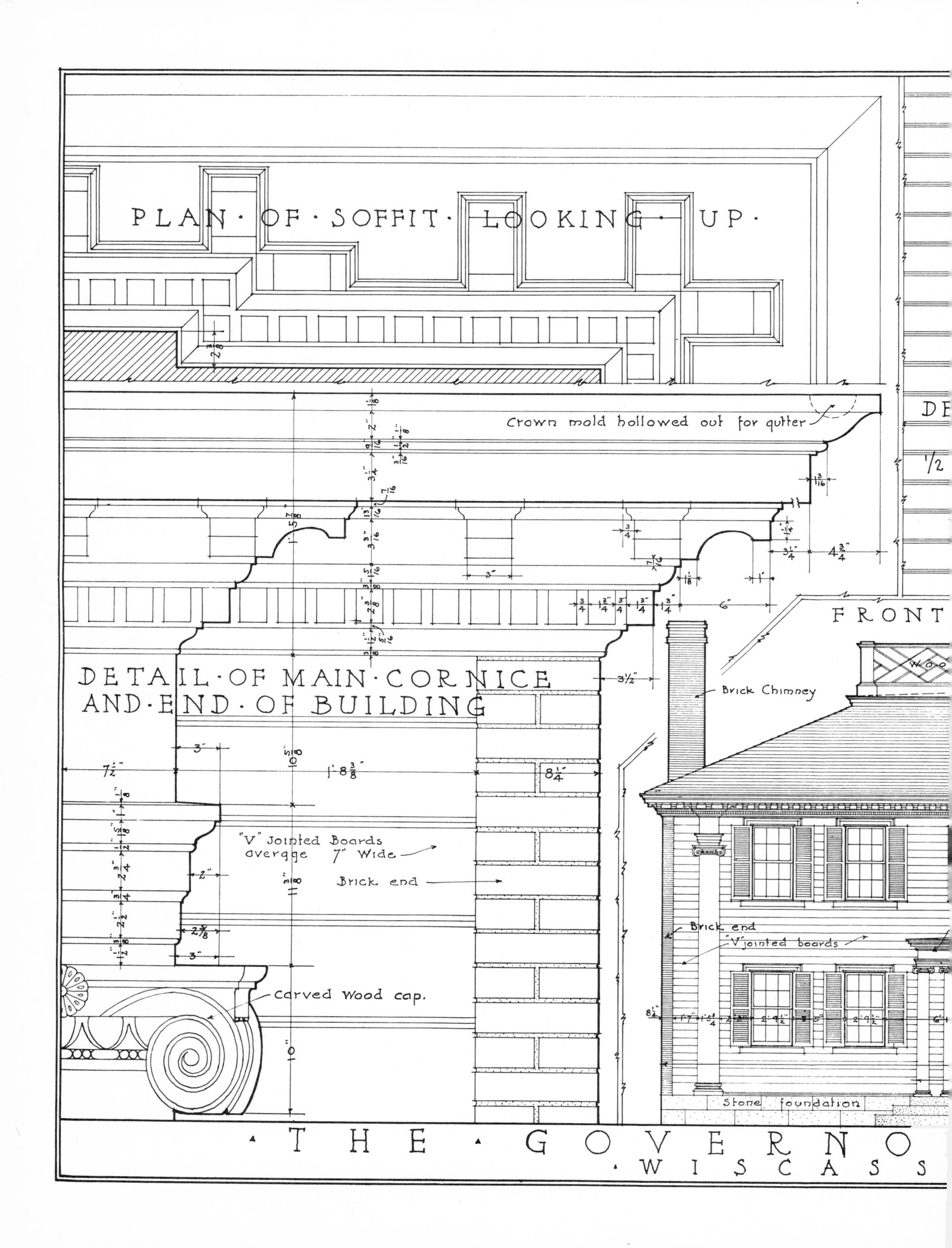
PLAN · OF · SOFFIT · LOOKING · UP ·
Crown mold hollowed out for gutter
DETAIL · OF · MAIN · CORNICE
AND · END · OF · BUILDING
"V" Jointed Boards
average 7" Wide
Brick end
Carved Wood cap.
Brick Chimney
FRONT
Brick end
"V" jointed boards
Stone foundation
· THE · GOVERNO
· WISCASS

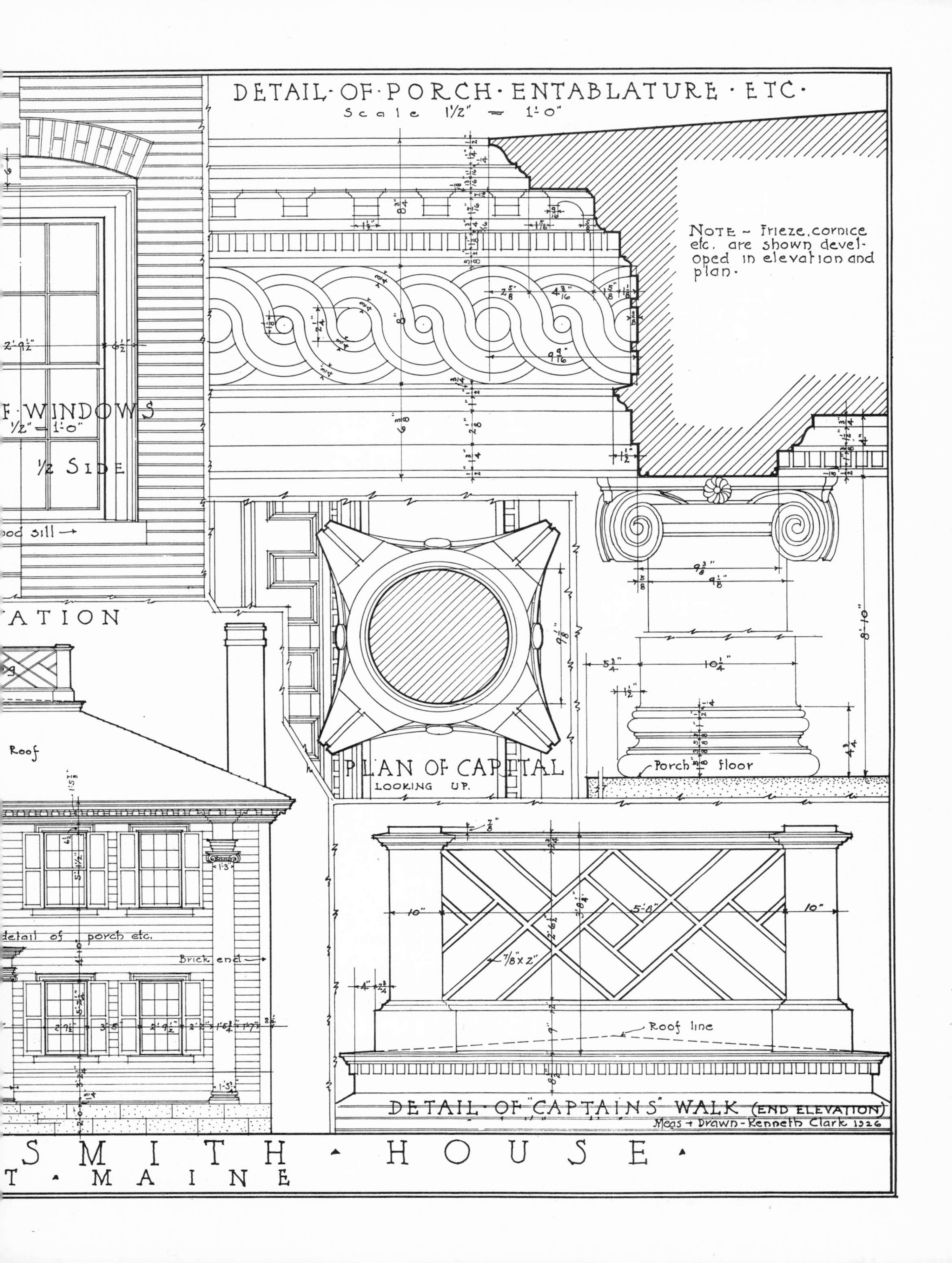
DETAIL·OF·PORCH·ENTABLATURE·ETC·
Scale 1½" = 1'-0"
NOTE ~ Frieze, cornice etc. are shown developed in elevation and plan.
PLAN OF CAPITAL
LOOKING UP.
Porch floor
F·WINDOWS
½" = 1'-0"
½ SIDE
ATION
Roof
detail of porch etc.
Brick end
Roof line
DETAIL·OF "CAPTAINS" WALK (END ELEVATION)
Meas + Drawn - Kenneth Clark 1926
SMITH·HOUSE·
T·MAINE

THE LEE-SMITH HOUSE, WISCASSET,
MAINE [BUILT ABOUT 1792]
*Now known as the Governor S. E. Smith House*

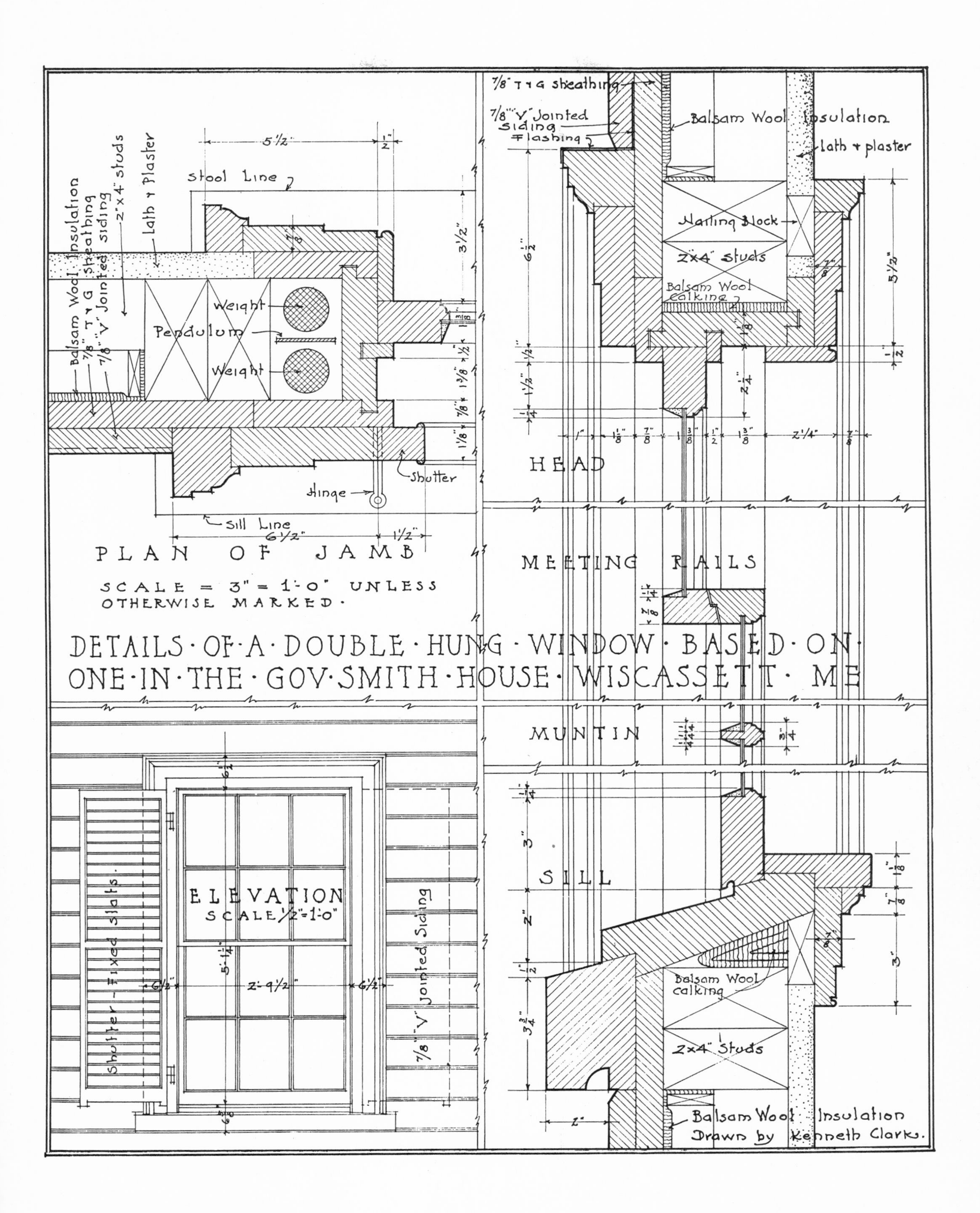
7/8" T + G sheathing
7/8" "V" Jointed siding
Flashing
Balsam Wool Insulation
Lath + plaster
Nailing Block
2x4" Studs
Balsam Wool calking
HEAD
MEETING RAILS
MUNTIN
SILL
Balsam Wool calking
2x4" Studs
Balsam Wool Insulation
Drawn by Kenneth Clark.
Balsam Wool Insulation
7/8" T + G Sheathing
7/8" "V" Jointed siding
2"x4" studs
Lath + Plaster
Stool Line
Weight
Pendulum
Weight
Shutter
Hinge
Sill Line
PLAN OF JAMB
SCALE = 3" = 1'-0" UNLESS OTHERWISE MARKED.
DETAILS · OF · A · DOUBLE · HUNG · WINDOW · BASED · ON · ONE · IN · THE · GOV · SMITH · HOUSE · WISCASSETT · ME
ELEVATION
SCALE 1/2"=1'-0"
Shutter - Fixed slats
7/8" "V" Jointed Siding

DETAIL OF FRONT PORCH

FRONT PORCH

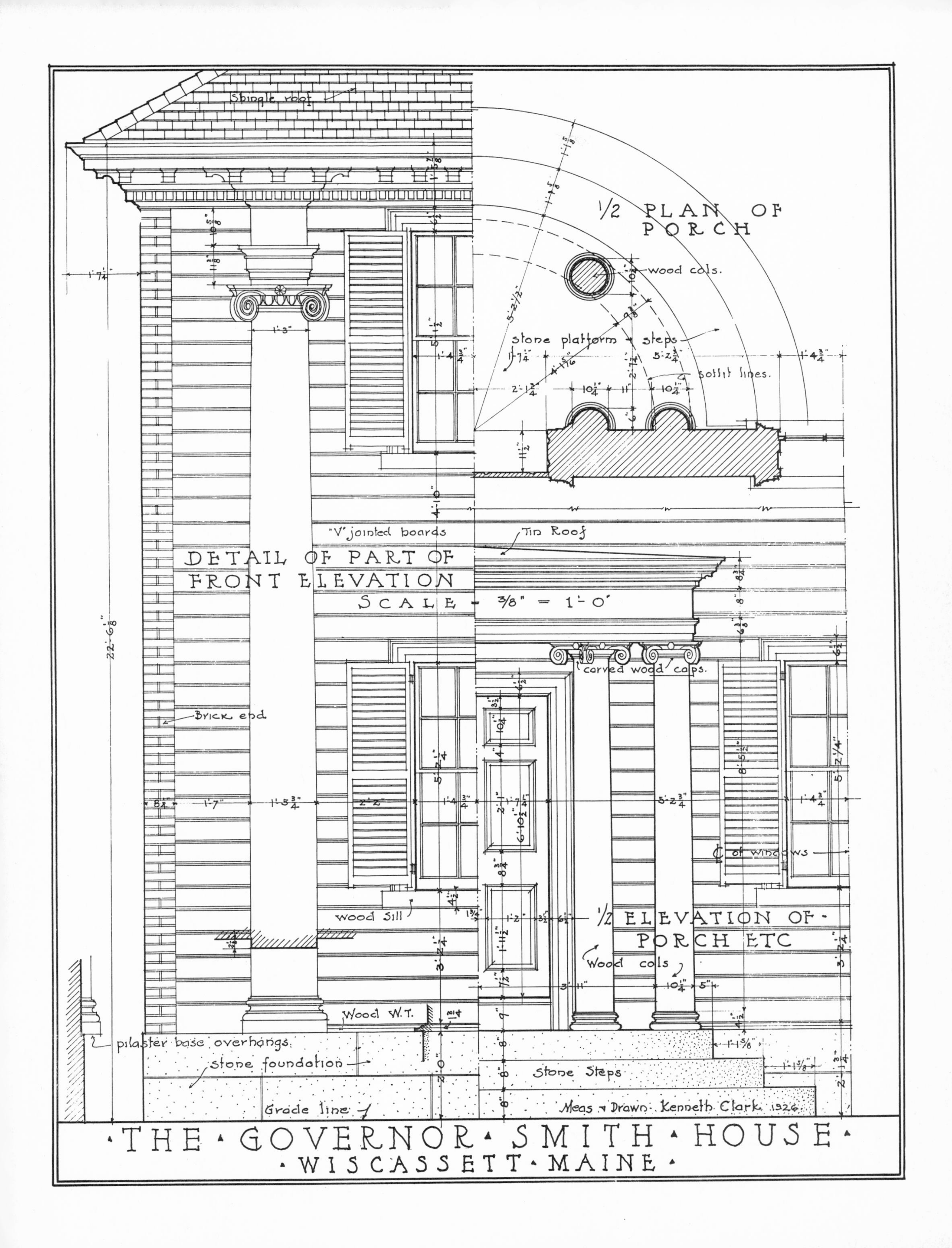


·THE·GOVERNOR·SMITH·HOUSE·

·WISCASSETT·MAINE·

THE NICKELS-SORTWELL HOUSE, WISCASSET, MAINE

THE NICKELS-
SORTWELL HOUSE,

DETAIL OF
MAIN FACADE

DETAIL OF ENTRANCE HALL
THE NICKELS-SORTWELL HOUSE, WISCASSET, MAINE

THE ABIEL WOOD HOUSE, WISCASSET, MAINE

THE CLAPP HOUSE, WISCASSET, MAINE

Main Hall and Stairway Looking toward Front Door

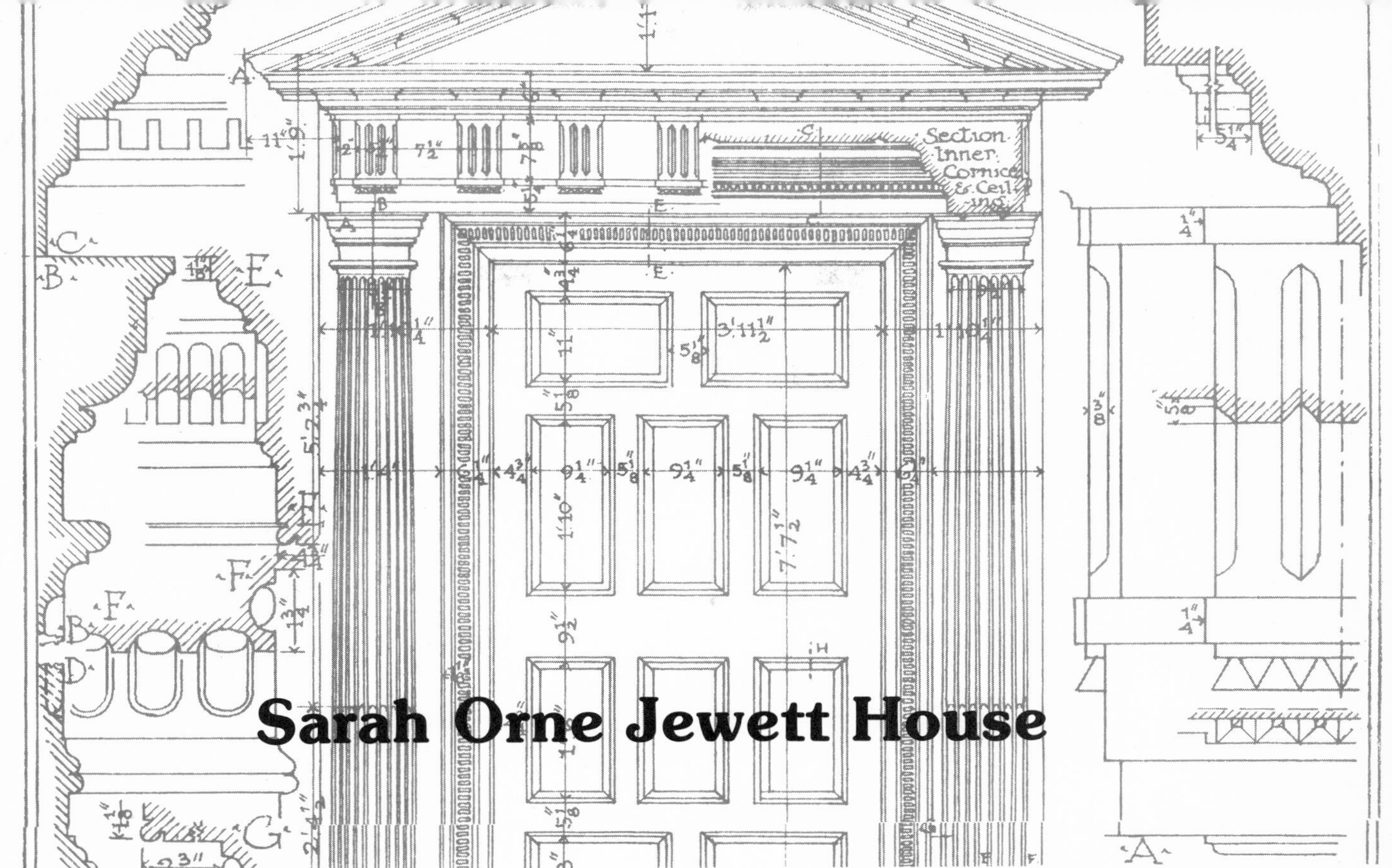


# Sarah Orne Jewett House

AMONG the areas "set apart" from the older township of Kittery in 1713 is the land that was again subdivided, a century later, in 1814, into Berwick, North Berwick and South Berwick—which is the present name of what was the old village or original town settlement upon the Maine side of the river from Salmon Falls, now in New Hampshire. In this Kittery section, as in so many other parts of the region round about, the architecture stems from the old Portsmouth types, and the more important houses were probably built by the same builders who had "raised" the better places in Portsmouth—located at the mouth of the Piscataqua, and the "port" of the inland region back of it along "Great Bay" and the navigable stretches of the confluent rivers.

Some of the other old dwellings—and most of those earlier than the Jewett Mansion—have disappeared leaving this structure, which from the records kept by one Master Taite in an old journal, we know was built by John Haggins or Higgins. He wrote, "Mr. John Higgins raised a new house at the turn of the ways near Mr. Robert Rodgers on Berwick side on Thursday, April ye 7th, 1774." When Hamilton House was built a year later—lower down on the same side of the river, with its own wharf and warehouses—it was directed to be "larger than John Haggins' house." Hamilton House is the single other fine Mansion remaining in this part of the Township, to maintain the Portsmouth tradition; the Judge Haynes house, set high upon its steep-rising hillside on the road to York, being of a later and quite different type. Of the builder, John Haggins or Higgins, little has been discovered, except that it is known he loved convivial company, his pipe and his toddy, and probably spent many a night at the town Inn, from which, tradition says, his wife Nancy had often to drag him, when the nine o'clock bell rang! Years later, the property passed into the hands of Captain Theodore Jewett, whose son, Dr. Jewett, was well patronized in the countryside, judging by the eight granite hitching posts and horse block that remain today. He was the father of Mary and Sarah Orne Jewett.

The house is large and square, with the end roof slopes far steeper than those to front and back—a Portsmouth peculiarity that also marked the roof of another old house, formerly across the square nearby, but long since disappeared, and several old Portsmouth dwellings, including the Tobias Lear House (c. 1740), still standing just around the corner from the Wentworth-Gardner House (1760). The Jewett House, as it has now come to be known, is set rather near the street, with a gate (of somewhat older design than the present fence) opening upon the brick walk to the front door. The door is protected by an unusual pedimented porch, which is in turn overhung by old, crowding lilac shrubs, bordered by dwarf box.

The house fronts the village square. Older pictures show the house with what appears to be a balustraded "walk" along the roof ridge, but this was rather an ornamental roof cresting, of consider-

West End of Parlor (Southwest Room), First Floor

Hall Doorway, Looking into Southwest Parlor

The "Secret Stairway" Between the H
Rooms, Looking from Breakfast Room

Southeast Room, First Floor; Formerly Mary Jewett's Library

Northeast (Family Breakfast) Room, First Floor

General View
Across Town Square

General View from Southwest

ably later date. The original corner trim appears to have been quoins, later replaced by "cornerboards". The old-fashioned "Privy" and Laundry are at the extreme north end of the Ell, along with a capacious side entry and store room.

But it is in the main part of the house that the most architectural and sentimental interest remains. The Entrance Hall is unusually beautiful with many of the best details of the Portsmouth tradition gathered in this one example. The same finish is carried up into the second Hall, which reminds one particularly of the same space in the Wentworth-Gardner House, although lacking the large plaster cove. The heavy Cornice, Door Cap and entablature have caused the doors—particularly upon the second floor—to be kept very low; and both the first Hall archway, and window top on the staircase, have an unusually shaped and carved "Key" ornament. The staircase has other unusual features, along with the "reversed bracket run," used as a skirtboard along the stair dado, as elsewhere in Portsmouth dwellings of the same or earlier period. The local legend is that the finish of the stairs and the two Halls took two men one hundred days of labor to complete ("long" days, not the "union labor" hours of today!) The woodwork in the Hall, and in some other parts of the house, remained unpainted until 1838, when it had ripened to a beautiful tobacco brown tone.

The first floor room at the right, once Mary Jewett's Library, but now a Parlor furnished simply in the period of the rest of the house, contains an original fireplace treatment, without mantel shelf or the earlier "Bolection" moulding. Across the hall, on the southwest corner of the house, is the more elaborately detailed Parlor, a beautiful room, with the cornerposts converted into fluted pilasters after the Portsmouth fashion. A mantel, probably later in date, but finely worked by carpenter's chisel-carving, is notable in this room; and in the passage beside the fireplace connecting it with the Dining Room, are two simple, (and also later) glass cupboards, with glazed doors for the "best chiney." Here the finish and detail are much simpler. By crossing the hall back of the staircase into the Breakfast Room, a still earlier and sterner treatment—in accord with the old kitchen beyond—will be found. At the east of the chimney on this side of the house is the usual "Secret Staircase" that runs

Detail View of South Entrance Front

from here to the Attic floor two stories above. It is actually only the "Side Stairs" of Colonial tradition, but in this house lacks any outside doorway to the East. The old Dresser in the kitchen was formerly fitted with old blue Chinese Willow-ware.

On the second floor the stair rail is very high—appearing the more so from the low ceiling appearance due to the heavy hall cornice — but is gracefully curved in plan as well as ramped in elevation, at both the landing and end of the stairwell. This effect also partially duplicates that in the Wentworth-Gardner House. The two black Horsehair sofas, described in Laura E. Richards recollections of the house, still stand on either side at the front of the second Hall.

On this floor four bedrooms occupy the same locations as the rooms below, that in the southwest corner being again the most elaborate. Once more cornerposts, mantelpiece, dado, cornice, and door and window trim are fondly elaborated — chisel-cut and hand-molded by carpenter's tools. This room belonged to Mary, and the one across the Hall, on the southeast corner, with its simpler finish, was the Guestroom. Going through the passage beside the hidden stair, one comes to Sarah's room, which still contains its old Victorian

General View of House from Southeast
*(This view, taken in 1935, shows upper Roof Balustrade in position)*

General View of House from Northwest

Detail of Front Porch Column and Cornice

South Entrance Porch

North Entrance Doorway

furniture and arrangement, just as it was left by Sarah Jewett, even to the heavy green color of the paint! The room in the northwest corner, over the Dining Room, belonged to "Theodore," the nephew, Dr. Eastman, while north of Sarah's room opened the Bath, and beyond that was the servants' ell. The front door is large and unusually paneled, with huge wrought hinges, brass handle and knocker.

The attic was finished about 1870, to which period also belong the overlarge and aggressive dormers.

Many wall papers and curtains remain to display their Victorian traditions, even those spread out over the floor below the windows! The southwest bedroom still has a beautiful old maroon "flock" paper, patterned in worn white and silver mica. This paper was printed in 18 x 22 inch sections for a French Governor-General in the West Indies, but intercepted by a privateer and brought into Salem, where Capt. Jewett secured it. The other papers, while not as old, are in character with the house, its history, and the Victorian furniture of its famous occupants.

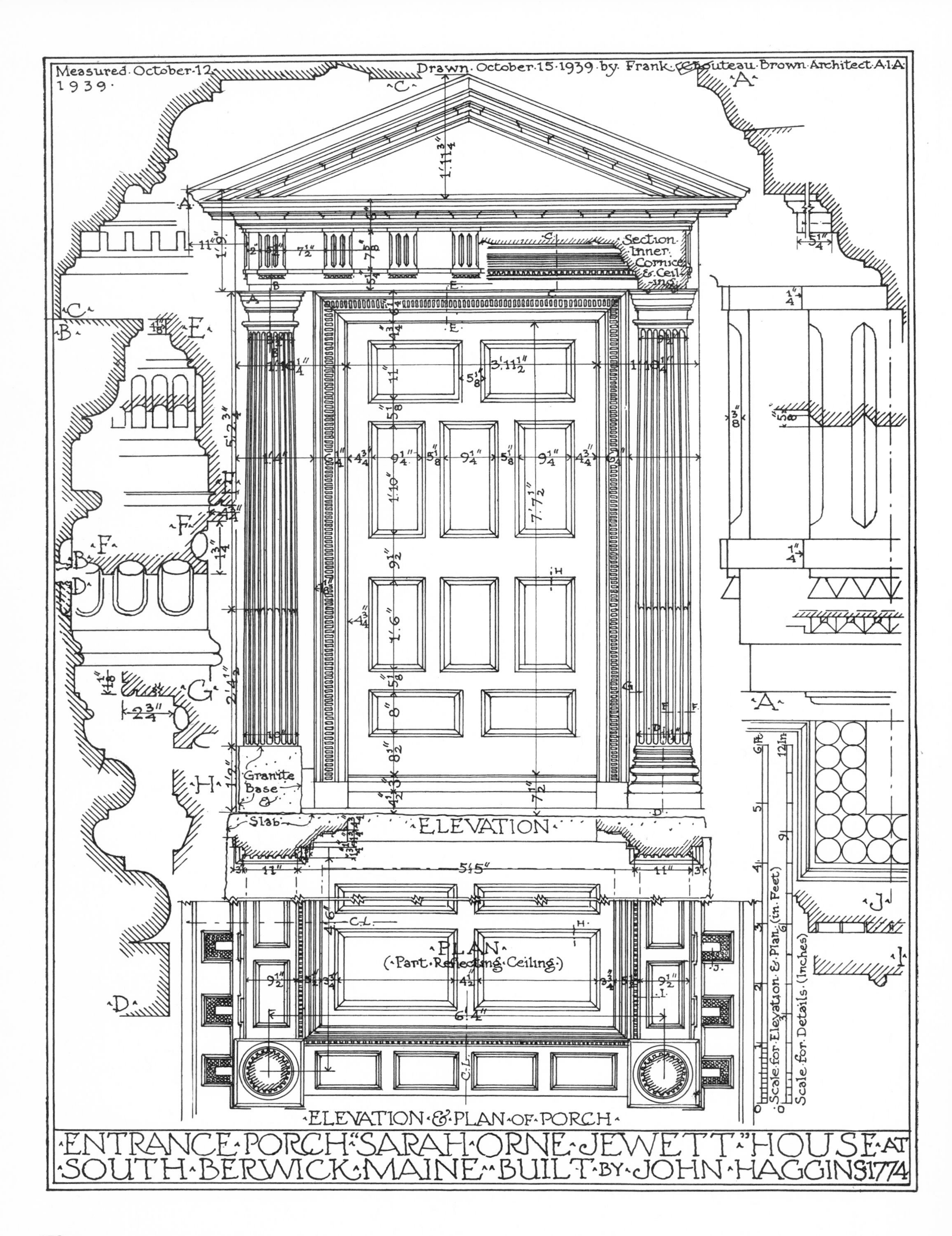
Measured October 12 1939
Drawn October 15 1939 by Frank Chouteau Brown Architect A.I.A.
Section Inner Cornice & Ceiling
Granite Base &
Slab
ELEVATION
PLAN
(Part Reflecting Ceiling)
Scale for Elevation & Plan (in Feet)
Scale for Details (Inches)
ELEVATION & PLAN OF PORCH
ENTRANCE PORCH "SARAH ORNE JEWETT" HOUSE AT
SOUTH BERWICK MAINE BUILT BY JOHN HAGGINS 1774

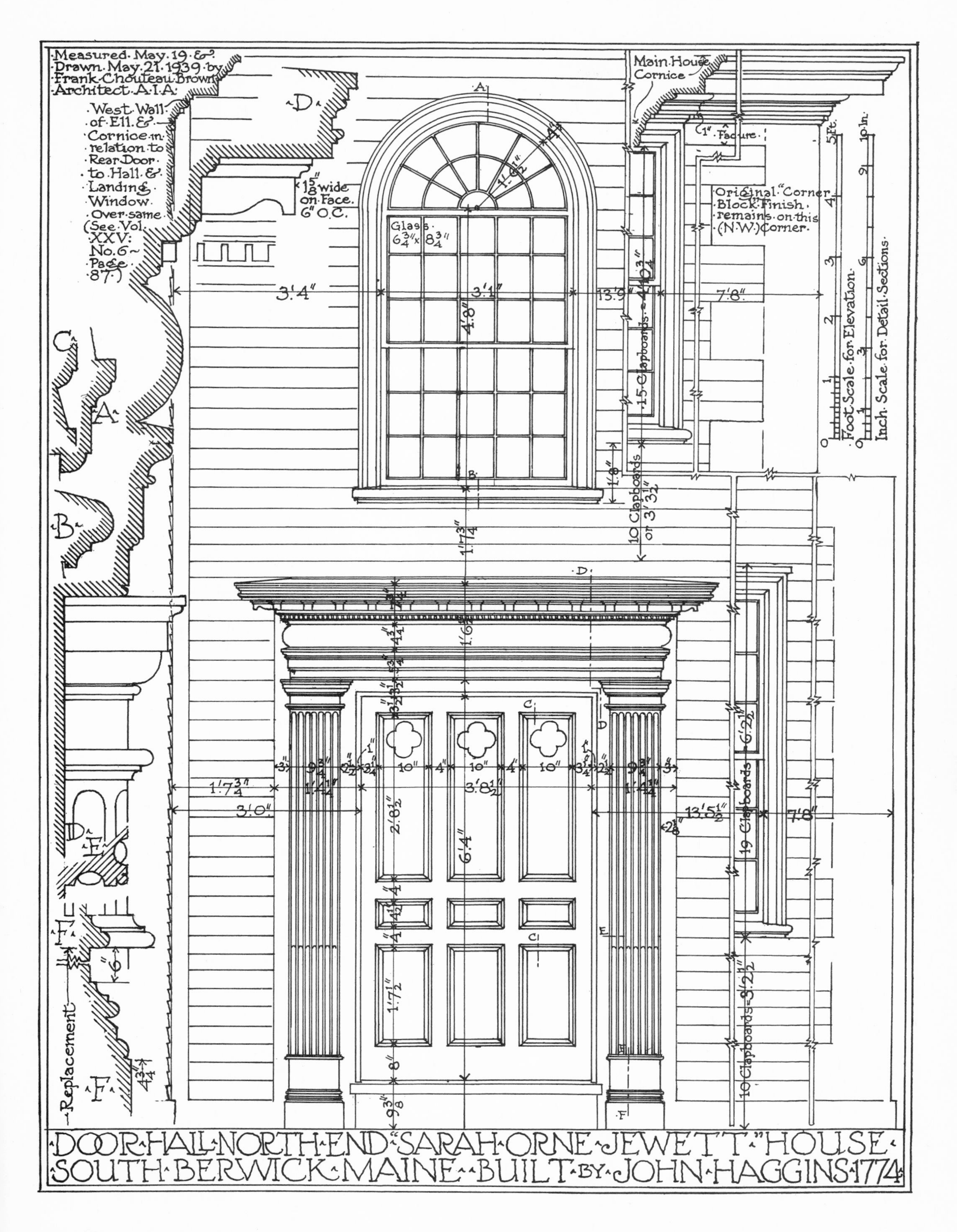
Measured May 19 & Drawn May 21 1939 by Frank Chouteau Brown Architect A.I.A.
West Wall of Ell & Cornice in relation to Rear Door to Hall & Landing Window Over same (See Vol. XXV: No. 6~ Page 87)
1⅝" wide on Face. 6" O.C.
Glass 6¾" x 8¾"
Main House Cornice
1" Facure
Original "Corner Block" Finish remains on this (N.W.) Corner.
Foot Scale for Elevation
Inch Scale for Detail Sections
15 Clapboards
10 Clapboards or 3'3½"
19 Clapboards
10 Clapboards = 3'2½"
Replacement
DOOR HALL NORTH END "SARAH ORNE JEWETT" HOUSE
SOUTH BERWICK MAINE BUILT BY JOHN HAGGINS 1774

Mantel in Southwest (Mary's) Bedroom

The Southwest Corner (Mary Jewett's) Bedroom

The Southeast Corner (Guest) Bedroom

Northwest (Dr. Theodore's) Bedroom

Southeast Bedroom Doorway,
Looking into Hall

West Side of Second Story Hallway

Northwest (Family Dining) Room, First Floor

Old Kitchen and Fireplace in North Ell

FRAMINGHAM ACADEMY—FRAMINGHAM, MASSACHUSETTS

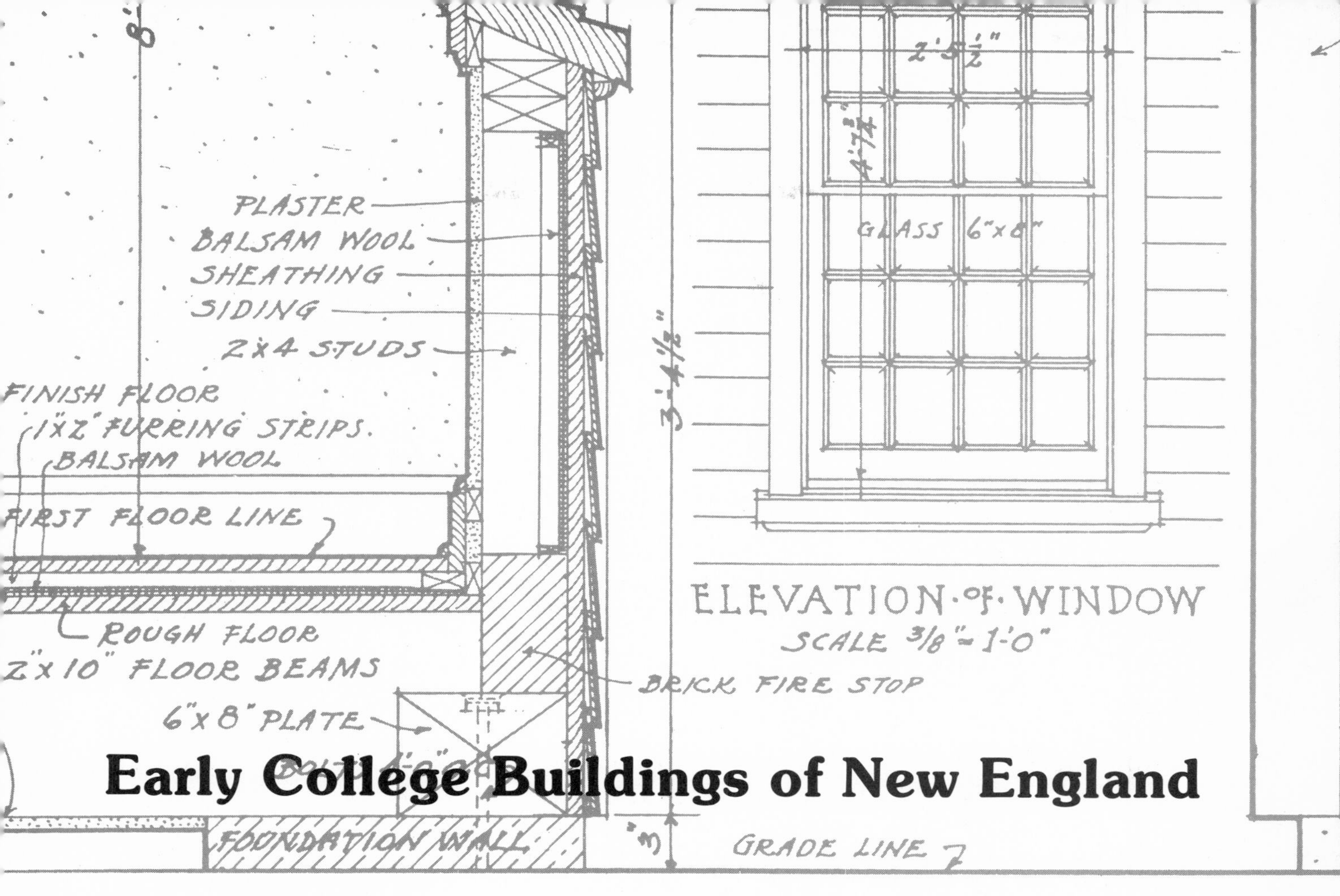


# Early College Buildings of New England

In many instances the original structures associated with the beginnings of early educational institutions in New England have long disappeared; or been superseded by later buildings, themselves already of considerable age and association. It was also the fact that in many cases the buildings first used for educational purposes were not especially constructed for that use; but merely adapted to the purpose. Classes for the younger children in the early colonies, in many locations in New England, usually known as "Dame Schools," were carried on in the homes of the "Dame" in whose charge the instruction of the children had been placed; or sometimes in another house more conveniently located, or of larger size, and therefore selected for the gathering of these small groups of local pupils of many varying ages.

No example of a small village schoolhouse, of an early date, especially built for the education of the younger scholars, is known still to exist in northern New England. A considerable number of one-room schoolhouse buildings may yet be found, scattered over some sections of Massachusetts, Rhode Island, Connecticut, Vermont, New Hampshire, and Maine—but usually they do not date from before 1830 to 1840. Some few have been kept nearly in their original condition (having been superseded by newer and larger buildings, and the "bus" system now in general use in rural communities having made them of no use on their original sites) but have been long closed and allowed to exist without care or repair. Many have disappeared, from fire or neglect, but a few still "carry on," remote and forlorn. Many more have been changed or adapted to other uses; perhaps to serve as a "Union Church"; made into a farm cottage; occasionally they have become "studios" for some summer artist; or have fallen to the use of a roadside stand or gas filling station!

One or two examples of these simple structures, that may be regarded as more or less representative of the "little old red schoolhouse" of storied tradition (although, as a matter of fact, about as often "white" as "red" in the locality here represented!) are illustrated in this number; one—now actually a "summer studio"—conveniently located adjacent to the dismantled remains of an old "town pump" was the first public schoolhouse of Rockport, Massachusetts!

New England early town records carry many stories of the old "Academies" that were founded in most towns of any importance; some of which languished for many years before the rising ascendency and success of the larger college institutions caused them to be abandoned. But a few have survived; some even flourishing today as accommodations for the younger scholars, in those localities where constant growth of surrounding towns and villages have made the need of an intermediate institution of this sort of continued neighborhood value. And two or three typical buildings illustrate this group of institutional architecture; the most pretentious being the three-story Derby Academy, in the old town of Hingham, in Massachu-

FIRST PUBLIC SCHOOLHOUSE, ROCKPORT, MASS.

SCHOOL AT GLOUCESTER, MASSACHUSETTS

setts, representative of the later and more prosperous structures of the period when these Academies most flourished; another being the original building (1763) of the little Academy founded and named after Lieut.-Governor Dummer, in Byfield, Massachusetts. Both these institutions are still flourishing and maintain a long record of educational ideals; although both now serve a far larger area than was ever contemplated as

DUMMER ACADEMY—ORIGINAL BUILDING 1763—BYFIELD, MASSACHUSETTS

GROUP OF BUILDINGS—AMHERST COLLEGE, AMHERST, MASSACHUSETTS

possible at the time of their foundation.

Of the old College buildings in this section, it must at once be acknowledged that the earliest buildings of the first Institutions founded for the inculcation of learning have long since disappeared! There is every probability that those first constructed entirely for this the Society for the Preservation of New England Antiquities for April, 1933, Vol. XXIII, No. 4; illustrated by some drawings of conjectural restorations of the first building at Harvard College, in Cambridge, made by Perry, Shaw & Hepburn, the "Old College," which was built in 1638 and finally destroyed in 1679.

DERBY ACADEMY, HINGHAM, MASSACHUSETTS

purpose must have followed examples established by earlier collegiate buildings of European precedent, particularly in England. Those especially interested in these earliest structures may be referred to the article by Professor Samuel E. Morison in the publication of It was modeled upon the sort of Tudor structure that may still be seen in some of the earlier Colleges in Cambridge, England.

But actually none of the earliest existing Collegiate structures to be found in New England exhibits any architectural Tudor characteristics — unless perhaps what are claimed as remainders of the old single "Studies" of the English Colleges—small rooms about 5′0″ x 8′0″—some of which are still to be seen in the present Hollis Hall, in Harvard (though now used as lavatories or closets), may be considered as such a survival!

As a matter of fact, Harvard University preserves more early buildings than are to be found in any other College among the northern New England states; in their original exterior aspect, at least. It is acknowledged that the changes caused by accident, fire, wear, and usage have left little of their interior finish or structure in original condition. Among its earlier buildings are Massachusetts Hall, 1720; Hollis Hall, 1763; Harvard Hall, 1766; Stoughton Hall, 1805; Holworthy Hall, 1812; and Holden Chapel, 1744. All these are built of brick, and are representative of their periods, only Harvard Hall having been very much altered upon its exterior by later changes and additions. The yard also boasts of University Hall, the fine granite structure designed by Charles Bulfinch.

Brown University in Providence has preserved three of its first structures, University Hall, 1773; Hope College, 1825; and Manning Hall, the latter a fine example of the Greek revival influence, dating from 1833. Some of the other smaller Colleges have also kept one or two of their earlier buildings, though generally of later date than those listed.

Both at Cambridge and Providence, the buildings dating from before the Revolution were used during the war as barracks for soldiers; and at Harvard, both Massachusetts and Hollis have been largely rebuilt inside, having been used both for recitation rooms and dormitories at different times. Fires have also damaged the interiors of parts of these buildings, causing new firewalls to be installed, and many minor changes in stairways and interior partitions have had to be made from time to time.

These same factors have even extended to affect most of the structures dating from early in the Nineteenth Century; and have in some cases even altered their exterior appearance; as has been the case with several of the older buildings at Phillips Andover

ABBOTT HALL, ABBOTT ACADEMY—1829—ANDOVER, MASSACHUSETTS

PEARSON HALL—1817—PHILLIPS ANDOVER ACADEMY, ANDOVER, MASSACHUSETTS
*Charles Bulfinch, Architect*

UNIVERSITY HALL, HARVARD UNIVERSITY—1815—CAMBRIDGE, MASSACHUSETTS
*Charles Bulfinch, Architect*

Academy, for instance. Here no less than four of the existing buildings were designed by Bulfinch; but it is obvious, from any close study of the structures themselves, that their present state exhibits evidence that many changes—sometimes of considerable importance—have been made at various times to affect their fabric and exterior appearance. In the case of these particular structures, for instance, the belfries or cupolas are obviously not in their original relation to the designs. A large part of Pearson Hall, on both principal façades, show considerable areas of brickwork of a different period from the rest of the building; and several of the entrances exhibit evidences of changes and alterations that may have extensively varied their exterior appearance.

In general, however, despite changes in openings and roof lines; the additions of dormers, roof balustrades, or cupolas; these early College buildings, among the most interesting records of early brick masonry that have been preserved from Eighteenth Century periods, may be used to demonstrate the record in this particular. In every case, they exhibit an interest of texture that—secured by the use of irregular brick units, early bond variations, and varied joint treatments—contains material for the study and consideration of architects appreciative of maintaining the variety and values of historic periods of craftsmanship in masonry, or to avail themselves of the inherited traditions of that trade, and apply them to modern problems of architectural design.

Structures dating from the earlier years of the Nineteenth Century, on the other hand, exhibit another aspect, also valuable and suggestive to the modern designer. A study of the several buildings by Charles Bulfinch, for instance—and perhaps most particularly the building at Phillips Andover called by his name—is illuminating from the severity and chastity of their design, as well as the extreme simplicity and reserve of their molding treatment and ornamental embellishment.

Very probably this may have been the result of the requirement of economy imposed upon their designer by the conditions under which he was working at the time; of the need of these institutions to secure the utmost possible amount of building for the least possible amount of expenditure (a problem not very far removed from that confronting the profession during these very current years of the Twentieth Century!). But, whatever the cause, the results secured have great interest and value for architectural designers today. For interests of texture in the wall, other values have been substituted that may not be as widely interesting or appealing; for the romantic tendencies evident in the earlier designs, there are now to be seen the greater fineness and reserve of a Greek-derived delicacy and precision of outline and composition of area that approaches "bareness." The resulting simplicity certainly requires more understanding and a finer appreciation of the problem of architectural design upon the part of the public than might have been expected to exist at that time, even in New England. Or it may be that it was a direct outgrowth of the very social conditions then animating this section of North America; the natural expression in architecture of the civilization then being derived from the early years of the Republic; of the conditions of life and living then surrounding the developing mentality of the region that was to flower a little later in the school of literature and thought that was to achieve its fullest culmination in New England in the philosophy of Alcott, Thoreau, and Emerson!

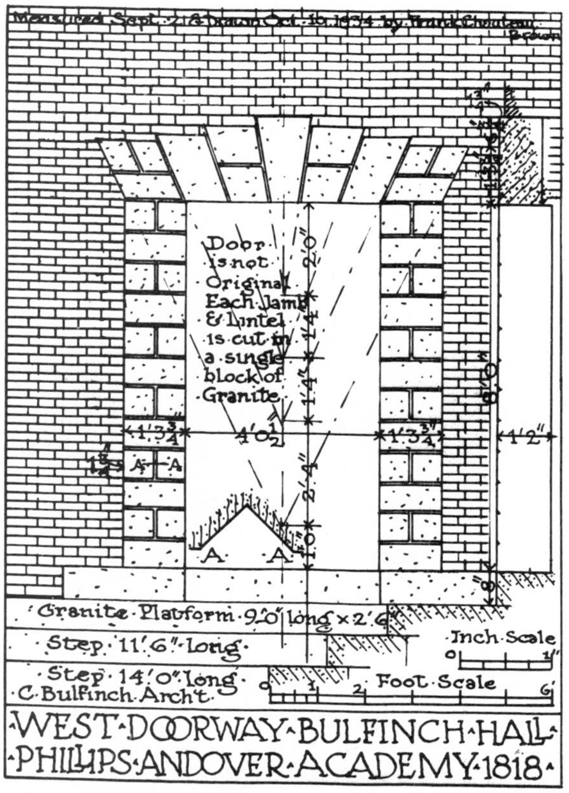

WEST·DOORWAY·BULFINCH·HALL·
·PHILLIPS·ANDOVER·ACADEMY·1818·

GRIFFIN HALL, WILLIAMS COLLEGE, WILLIAMSTOWN, MASSACHUSETTS

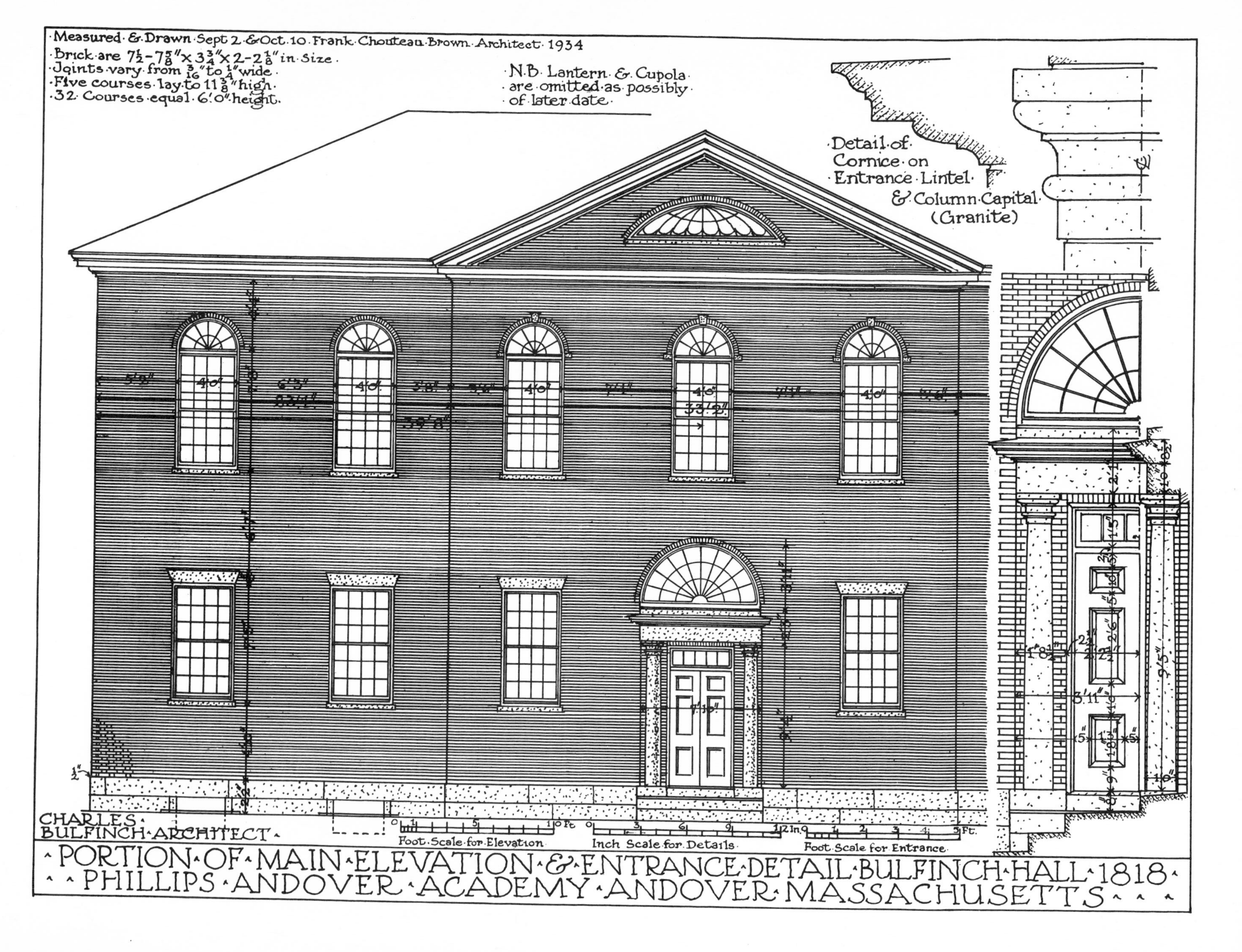

Measured & Drawn Sept 2 & Oct 10 Frank Chouteau Brown Architect 1934
Brick are $7\frac{1}{2}$-$7\frac{5}{8}$" x $3\frac{3}{4}$" x 2-$2\frac{1}{8}$" in Size
Joints vary from $\frac{3}{16}$" to $\frac{1}{4}$" wide
Five courses lay to $11\frac{3}{8}$" high
32 Courses equal 6'0" height
N.B. Lantern & Cupola are omitted as possibly of later date
Detail of Cornice on Entrance Lintel & Column Capital (Granite)
CHARLES BULFINCH ARCHITECT
Foot Scale for Elevation
Inch Scale for Details
Foot Scale for Entrance
PORTION OF MAIN ELEVATION & ENTRANCE DETAIL BULFINCH HALL 1818
PHILLIPS ANDOVER ACADEMY ANDOVER MASSACHUSETTS

BULFINCH HALL, PHILLIPS ANDOVER ACADEMY—1818—ANDOVER, MASSACHUSETTS

*Charles Bulfinch, Architect*

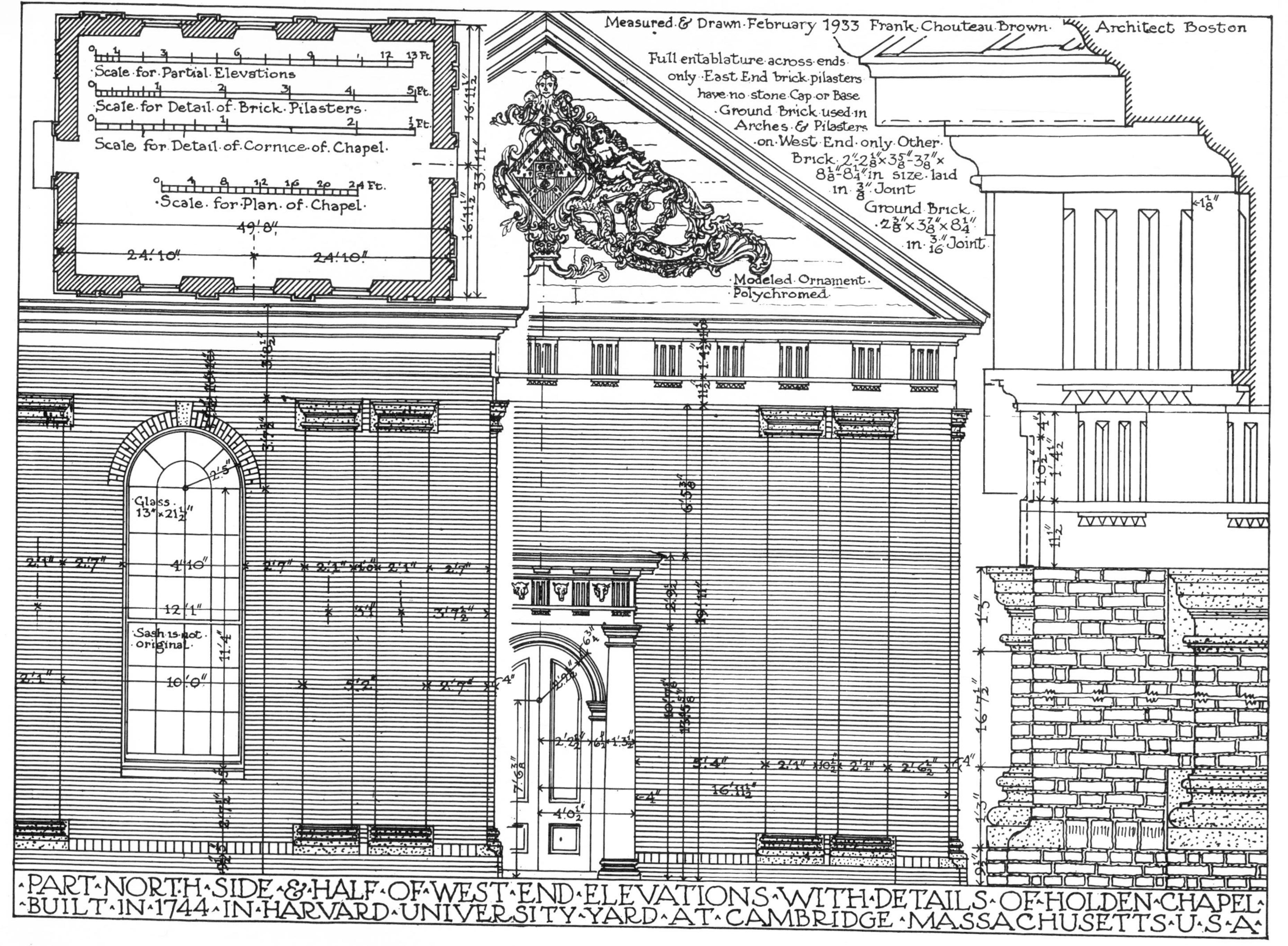
Measured & Drawn February 1933 Frank Chouteau Brown Architect Boston
Full entablature across ends only East End brick pilasters have no stone Cap or Base
Ground Brick used in Arches & Pilasters on West End only Other Brick 2"-2 1/8" x 3 5/8"-3 7/8" x 8 1/8"-8 1/4" in size laid in 3/8" Joint
Ground Brick 2 3/8" x 3 7/8" x 8 1/4" in 3/16" Joint
Modeled Ornament Polychromed
Scale for Partial Elevations
Scale for Detail of Brick Pilasters
Scale for Detail of Cornice of Chapel
Scale for Plan of Chapel
Glass 13" x 21 1/2"
Sash is not original
PART NORTH SIDE & HALF OF WEST END ELEVATIONS WITH DETAILS OF HOLDEN CHAPEL
BUILT IN 1744 IN HARVARD UNIVERSITY YARD AT CAMBRIDGE MASSACHUSETTS U S A

HOLDEN CHAPEL, HARVARD UNIVERSITY—1744—CAMBRIDGE, MASSACHUSETTS

HOUSE AT STONINGTON, CONNECTICUT.
Pedimented doorway with square-headed opening.

# ways

comparative study, the illustrations have been grouped in eight classes, in accordance with the simplicity of their design rather than in order of age, or grouped according to locality. Of these divisions the simplest is obviously the square-headed opening without transom or side

ıt elaboration in the treatment.
lustrations happen to show an
ıordinary antiquity (for this
arliest being the doorway of the
"se, at Water Mill, Long Island,
, in which a common enough
ablature treatment has been
ıg the shaft of the pilaster by a
ıembling lattice, and applied to
g of the door frame. This
done at any time in Colonial
ıe frontispiece was very clearly
Colonial architects to be a
: and not a structural one
from structural forms), and
re willing and accustomed to
*applied* motives which they
took with genuine structural members: which is to my mind an indication of genuine understanding of architecture, in contradistinction to the late Italian architects, who were accustomed to ornament and distort structural members so that they appeared, and sometimes were, unstable. A more significant in-

House in Norwichtown, Connecticut.
1802.

House near Westbrook, Connecticut.
1795.

DOORWAYS—GROUP "A"
SQUARE-HEADED OPENING
WITHOUT TRANSOM OR SIDE LIGHTS.

Anna Halsey House, Water Mill, Long Island.
1690.

Stephen Bockers House, Norwich, Connecticut.
1700.

Webb House, East Marion, Long Island.
1702.

DOORWAYS—GROUP "B"
SQUARE-HEADED OPENING
WITH RECTANGULAR TRANSOM.

House at Wells, Maine.
Circa 1815.

dication of the age of the doorway is the fact that the entire entablature is broken around the projection of the pilasters, for it will be found in all seventeenth-century work that there exists a tendency to break horizontal courses around all projections (compare the Deerfield door and the Marblehead door in a manner which can only be explained as a survival of the Gothic habit of breaking every label mold and belt course around every vertical member, no matter how insignificant, instead of letting them be received one by the other, or by butting them in part and returning them in part. That the Gothic influence did persist to some little extent in the Colonies is obvious to the student of early American architecture; the oldest extant building of English origin in the United States is unmistakably Gothic (St. Luke's Church at Smithfield, Va.), and characteristic Gothic moldings and even flamboyant tracery are found in even late work of the Dutch colonists on the Hudson River. The tendency to break all moldings around projections common to all seventeenth-century work persisted until the beginning of the nineteenth century among the Dutch, as in the case of the exquisite doorway of the Vreeland house in Englewood, N. J., illustrated on this page, although in all work of the English colonists it had long disappeared, or is found in sporadic cases only. The development of ornamental detail in England presents an entirely analogous case, the complicated character of the early Renaissance under Elizabeth and James I merging into the broad simple treatment of the Georgian art. A better exposition of the development of Colonial art cannot be made than three illustrations of these square-headed doorways: the earliest charming because of its naiveté, free and graceful; the Norwichtown doorway, equally simple, but sophisticated and skillful, obviously the product of an architect who "knew how"; the third, which combines the extreme attenuation of the latest Colonial work with the moldings of the Greek revival, shows exactly how Colonial architecture began to merge into the first of our long series of modern renaissances. The examples are in themselves comparatively unimportant; what they show is necessary to be known by every architect who hopes to approximate the beauty of Colonial work.

DOORWAY, CHASE HOUSE, ANNAPOLIS, MARYLAND.

That square-headed doorways were susceptible of considerable variation within narrow limits is sufficiently proved by the next three pages of three plates each. What has before been said applies equally to them, from the quaint door of the Webb house at East Marion, L. I., to the door of the Bishop Porter house; this latter I regard as being as nearly perfect as architecture can be, the fine flower of two centuries of effort in a single style. Simple in the extreme, it resembles the English work of the Adam style with less ornament, but in proportion in scale and in detail it cannot be surpassed.

Of the pedimented doorways it is necessary to say but little. The cushion frieze was a marked feature of all early work, usually appearing before 1750 and rarely after that date. The Griswold house is a late example if the date is correct; but dates on most Colonial work must be regarded as approximations, for unless well authenticated records appear the present owners rely on tradition and frequently confuse dates of original construction

DOORWAY, VREELAND HOUSE, ENGLEWOOD, N. J.

HOUSE AT FARMINGTON, CONNECTICUT.
Doorway with circular pediment over square-headed opening. Built in 1690.

House at Wells, Maine.
Circa 1815.

Farm House at Milton, Massachusetts.
1795.

DOORWAYS—GROUP "C"
SQUARE-HEADED OPENING
WITH CIRCULAR TRANSOM.

Bishop Porter House, Deerfield, Massachusetts.
1803.

House at Deerfield, Massachusetts.
Seventeenth century.

Miller House, Millers Place, Long Island.
1700.

DOORWAYS—GROUP "D"
PEDIMENTED WITH
SQUARE-HEADED OPENING.

Griswold House, Guilford, Connecticut.
Circa 1780.

Colonel Smith House, Stonington, Connecticut.
1800.

House at Apponaug, Rhode Island.
Circa 1800.

Stone House, Worthington, Massachusetts.
1803.

DOORWAYS—GROUP "E"
PEDIMENTED WITH
CIRCULAR HEADED OPENING.

DETAIL OF DOORWAY. HOUSE AT APPONAUG, RHODE ISLAND.
Built circa 1800.

and rebuilding, so that one can never be perfectly sure about any feature of a Colonial house unless it appears in some contemporary picture; and often assigned dates are obviously incorrect. However, care has been taken to distinguish those dates which are reasonably certain from those which are doubtful. Thus a circular headed opening within an order is a late development, and when appearing (as it sometimes does) on an old house must be regarded as an alteration, and not as dating from the original house, and while circular pediments undoubtedly occurred in every early work they were over square-headed openings. The broken pediment (of which three interesting examples are shown) was also of late date, that in Norwichtown, Connecticut, being perhaps the most interesting illustration, because of the curious series of breaks which are introduced into the moldings, both horizontal and rake, for no reason except their supposed decorative effect.

The combination of door and side lights, or door side lights and transom, is again of late development, probably not occurring commonly in New England before 1760 or 1770, although in Maryland excellent examples of far earlier date occur.

To sum up: the earliest doorways now known were undecorated in any way; the first decorated doorways are comparable in design to English Jacobean, showing traces of Gothic influence in their transitional style; succeeding them came a great mass of work which was fairly close to book classic proportions, with detail copied, as nearly as the limitations of the workmen allowed, from Roman precedent; next the extremely attenuated architecture comparable to English Adam, although I think it to have been a parallel development and not a derivative; and last a mixture of this style with Greek moldings and detail. This is of course true of all Colonial work, but nowhere can its development be so clearly traced as in the doorways.

Early Pine Circular-Top Open Corner Cupboard
HARTWELL FARMHOUSE, LINCOLN, MASSACHUSETTS

# Corner Cupboards

AFTER the Kitchen Dresser, or Wall Cupboard, so useful and necessary an adjunct to the early habitation in the Colonies that it seems almost to have been an initial fitment of every early dwelling,—the Corner Cupboard seems to have been next in demand by early housewives. And as the former was always located against the wall nearest the Kitchen fireplace, the latter was usually so placed as to fill up an internal angle in the least used corner of the Dining Room. The former was an actual necessity to keep at hand the cooking utensils needed in the kitchen, and the latter was almost equally necessary to at once protect and display the few family heirlooms of pewter or china, of which the housewife was most proud. The early Colonial

Open Corner Cupboard, with Scalloped Semi-Circular Top
DANIEL GOULD HOUSE,
BOXFORD, MASSACHUSETTS

"Corner Cupboard" was, indeed, the direct family ancestor of the ugly Victorian corner "Whatnot" of more recent memory!

Farther south it seems often to have been known as the "*Beau fait*," or "Buffet"; but along the northern coast it usually took a less pretentious name and form;—and, while retaining the fine proportions and outlines of its southern counterpart, it was generally made of more modest materials, and was better adapted to taking its place as an almost integral part of the walls of the Dining room. Where the finish was natural pine, so also we find the Corner Cupboard beautifully fitted into this atmospheric background; or, if the walls of the room were painted and paneled—or even plastered—we continue to find that one or another varied treatment of the well-known arched-top motive is appropriate, and even unobtrusively decorative—in a quiet New England way!—in some unused but conveniently visible corner of the daily family habitat.

Corner Cupboard in Old Manse
DEERFIELD, MASSACHUSETTS

Usually, in its simpler forms, the upper part of the cabinet was left open, with an arched, elliptical or segmental outline at the top; and the lower portion—up to about the height of the window sills or the room dado—had its shelves protected by paneled doors. Usually, the cupboard extended to the full height of the room,—fitting up against the ceiling, or into the beams or room cornice, in much the same way as did the early fireplace with overmantel treatment. But there were also simple corner treatments, with glazed or paneled doors shutting off the upper shelves from view, although by far the more customary and favorite design was to have the upper shelves protected by a glazed door or doors, with arched or segmental top, thus permitting objects placed upon the upper shelves easily to be seen at all times.

These glazed doors and arched tops were often enframed by a surrounding panel mould; or by side pilasters, tied into an entablature at the top; or fitting into the regular room cornice, whose mouldings would break out around or over the projecting pilasters or architraves flanking the opening. These pilasters were rather rarely of the full Georgian classic proportions,—but, in New England, were usually simpler and more attenuated, with but three or four flutings instead of the regulation seven, and often ended at top and bottom in other than the conventional cap and base of Classic precedent.

In plan, the problem of fitting shelving for the display of small objects was met by giving the cupboard a semi-circular back, and fitting the shelf outlines in the upper or more open part of the cupboard, to this circular plan, with the addition of a central projection at that point where the shelving was deepest. Sometimes—in the more elaborate examples—this circular top arch was filled

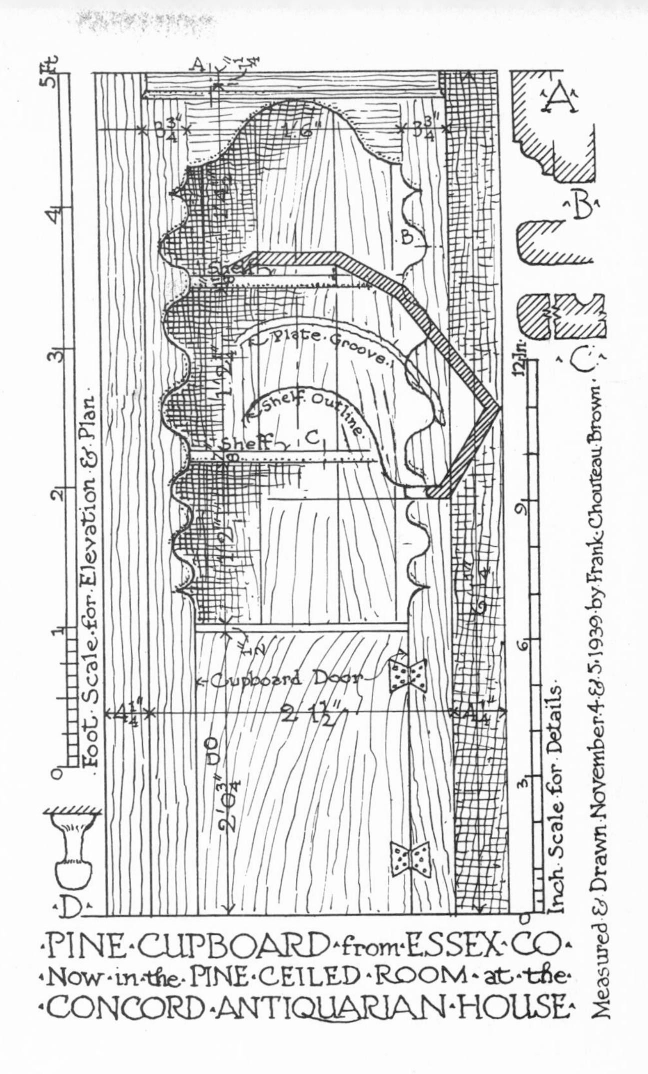


·PINE·CUPBOARD·from·ESSEX·CO·
·Now·in·the·PINE·CEILED·ROOM·at·the·
·CONCORD·ANTIQUARIAN·HOUSE·

Early Pine Corner Cupboard
*from* Essex County,
*Now in the* Antiquarian House *at*
CONCORD, MASSACHUSETTS

WIGGIN·VARNEY·HOUSE·STRATHAM·N·H· GEORGE·BLANCHARD·HOUSE·MEDFORD·
C·1770·CUPBOARD·IN·NATURAL·PINE
·MASS·1657-8·GLAZED·CORNER·CUPBOARD
Measured May 13 1938 & Drawn October 6 & 13 1940
by Frank Chouteau Brown Architect FAIA Boston
Measured in November 'J' 1932
Foot Scale for Elevations
Inch Scale for Details
Sash

Detail, Elevation View of Shell Top of Pine Corner Cupboard

WIGGIN-MILLER HOUSE,
STRATHAM, NEW HAMPSHIRE

Pine Open Corner
Cupboard, with Shell Top

*Courtesy Historic American Buildings Survey*

Early
Corner Cupboard,
with Glazed Semi-
Circular-Top Door
GEORGE BLANCHARD
HOUSE, MEDFORD,
MASSACHUSETTS

Open Corner Cupboard,
with Segment-Arched Top
*From* HILDRETH HOUSE,
CONCORD, MASSACHUSETTS

*Now in Concord Antiquarian House*

*Now in Concord Antiquarian House*

Corner Cupboard, with
Circle Top Glazed Door
*From* DEACON THOMAS BARRATT
HOUSE, CONCORD, MASS.

Measured November 1 1939 & Drawn November 5 1939 by Frank Chouteau Brown A.I.A. Boston
Foot Scale for Plans & Elevations
Inch Scale for Details
(Brass)
From the HILDRETH HOUSE 1790
From Deacon THOMAS BARRATT HOUSE
TWO OLD CORNER CUPBOARDS "CONCORD" MASSACHUSETTS
NOW IN THE HOUSE OF THE CONCORD ANTIQUARIAN SOCIETY AT CONCORD MASSACHUSETTS U.S.A.

with a semi-domed treatment,—sometimes carried out in plaster, but more often in wood,—when the under part of this semi-dome was sometimes carved more or less skillfully into a conventional shell. The example from the Wiggin-Miller House has been executed in the simplest possible way, by moulding rather than actual carving the built-up wooden back of the cupboard.

This typical semi-circular plan and design of the corner cupboard, once fully developed, was found adaptable to locations other than the inner corner of a room. It could be used recessed within a flat paneled wall, sometimes covered with a "blind paneled door," that was itself almost a unit of the wall paneling. Some very elaborate examples have been designed to meet this sort of a location.

The cupboards here and on page 212 represent a type where perhaps some local carpenter was attempting to suggest the appearance of the shell-topped cupboard, by introducing this scalloped effect around the inner edge of the semi-circular outlined top of the upper recess. This is more probably the case with the example on page 212. That upon this page developing a sophistication and skill of design, that quite transcend any suggestion of shallow imitation.

Open Corner Cupboard, with Scalloped Semi-Circular Top
DANIELS HOUSE,
SOMERS, CONNECTICUT

Early Corner Cupboard,
with Open Arched Top
JABEZ WILDER HOUSE,
HINGHAM, MASSACHUSETTS

Recessed Wall Cupboard,
with Open Arched Top
TIMOTHY WOOD HOUSE,
HALIFAX, MASSACHUSETTS

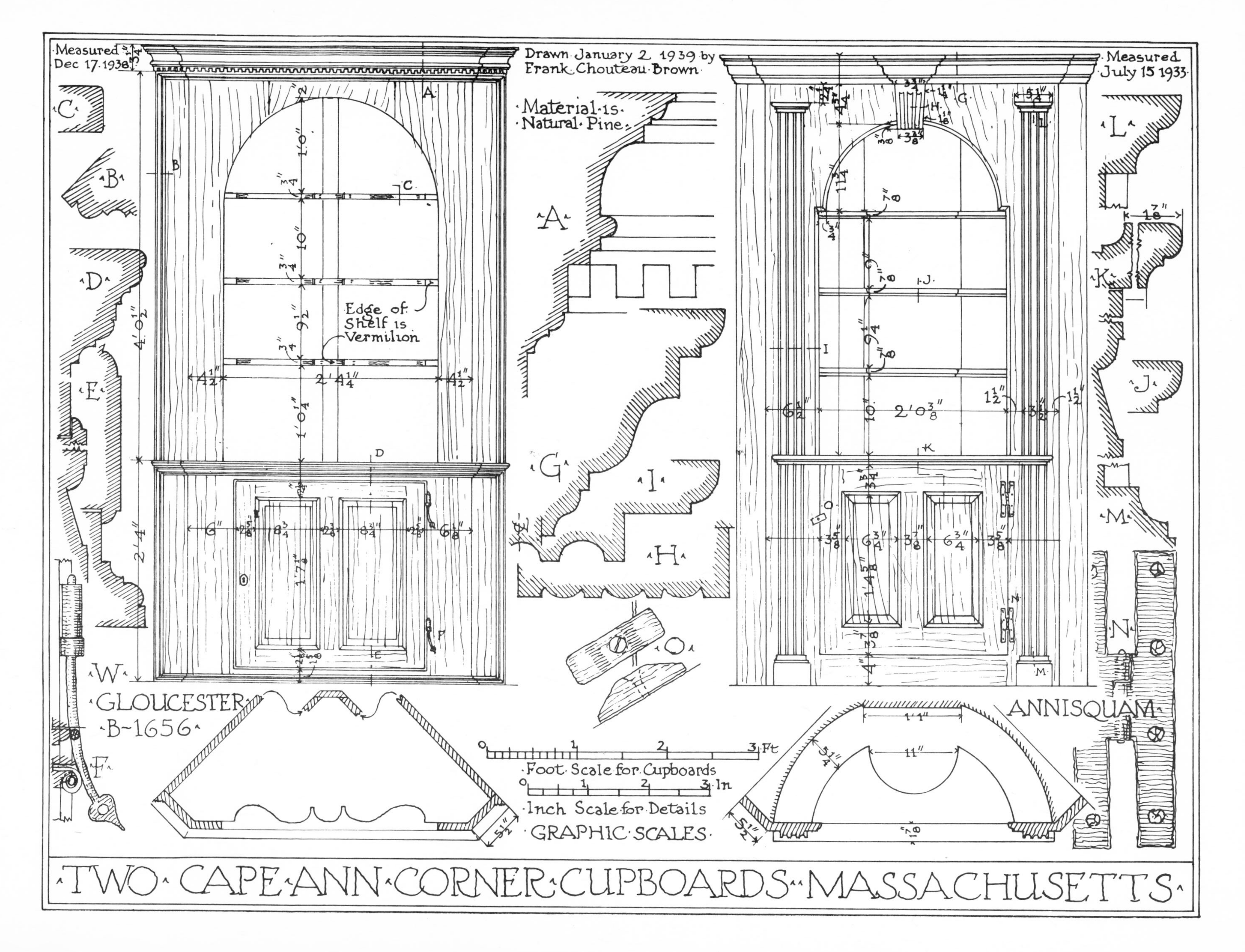
Measured Dec 17. 1938
Drawn January 2 1939 by Frank Chouteau Brown
Measured July 15 1933
Material is Natural Pine
Edge of Shelf is Vermilion
GLOUCESTER B-1656
ANNISQUAM
Foot Scale for Cupboards
Inch Scale for Details
GRAPHIC SCALES
TWO CAPE ANN CORNER CUPBOARDS MASSACHUSETTS

STRAIGHT-TOP CORNER CUPBOARD,
WITH PANELED DOORS
COL. ALEXANDER FIELD HOUSE,
LONGMEADOW, MASS.

The straight-top type shown here is of less usual design. The unusual width of the design,—as well as the use of paneled doors to enclose the upper shelving, indicates definite reticence and individuality on the part of its builders.

Most of the examples shown here are early types, some—as in the George Blanchard House—being original to the structure. In many cases these early examples can be identified by the use of a "bolection" moulding around the arched top or along the sides of the opening. In other cases, what was originally a very simple and primitive design, has been later supplemented by pilasters or other extensions, until it has become more pretentious,—and its actual age and integrity somewhat obscured in the process.

It should be remembered that, because of the decorative and appealing character of the corner cupboard, it has very often been separated from its original place of building. A family sells an old homestead, but reserves a mantel or two, as well as their old Corner Cupboard. As a rule, the earliest Cupboards were built for houses with low ceilings; and consequently, when a Cupboard is of somewhat lesser height than the room of which it is now a part,—one may suspect it to have been originally built for another house than that in which it is now placed. Of course, that must always be the case when they are preserved in some Museum or Historical Society,—although that fact will also the more generally guarantee the authenticity of their local origin. In so many instances has the corner cupboard been transposed from its original to another location, that it is unreliable to expect its date to be the same as that of the house in which it may now be placed.

That this is not always the case, is proved by the Cupboard in the Norton House at Annisquam, which was found by the present owners built into one of the upstairs room corners, and removed by them—for greater usefulness—to the lower story,—

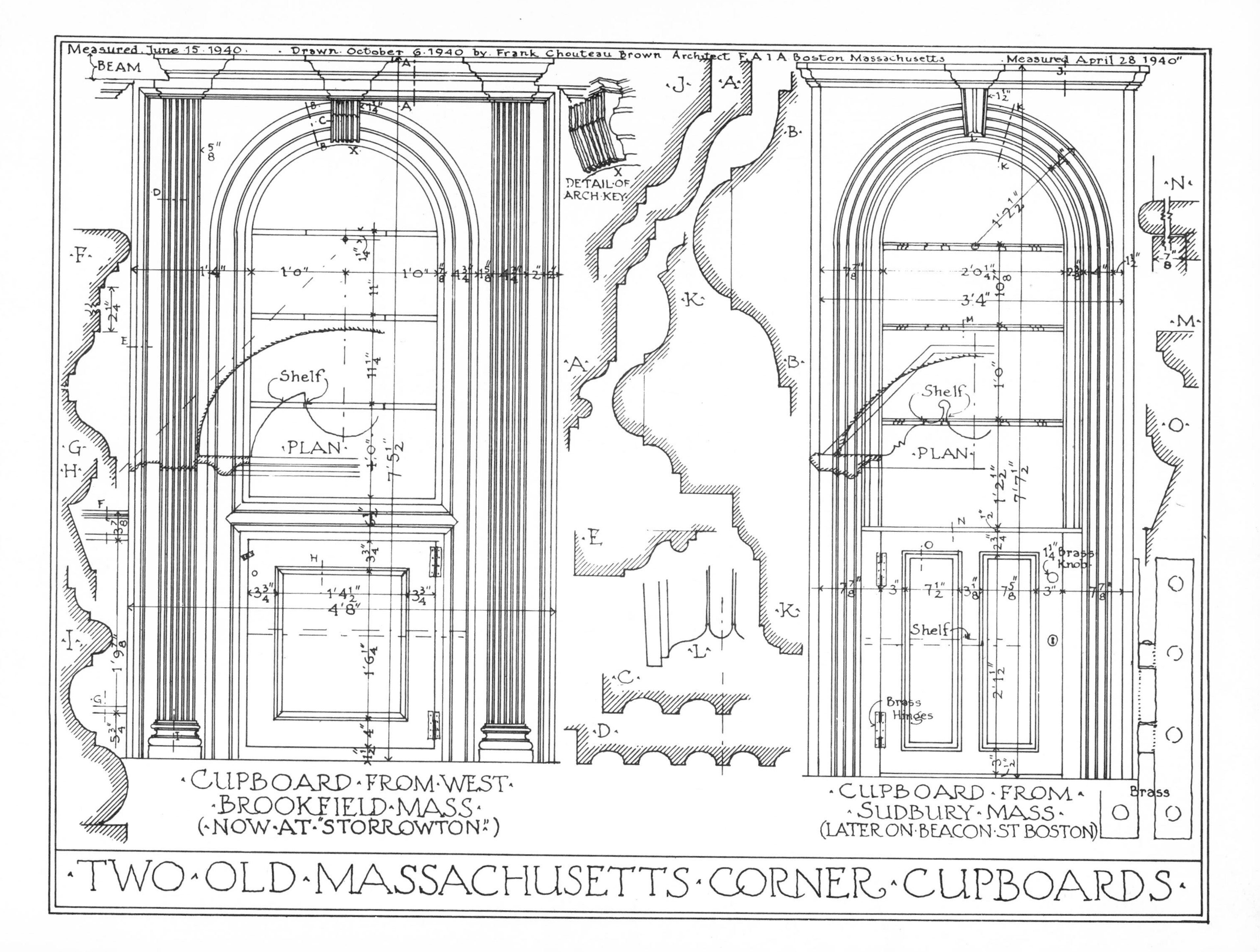


TWO OLD MASSACHUSETTS CORNER CUPBOARDS

Open Corner Cupboard, Now in Phillips House, "Storrowton," Massachusetts

Open Corner Cupboard, Now in Gilbert House, "Storrowton," Massachusetts

Corner Cupboard from Sudbury, Mass.

where it now shows of less height than the ceiling of the room where it is located. To the writer's knowledge, just half of the cupboards here illustrated came from other houses than those in which they are now located. But their removal often has been the cause of their preservation down to the present day,—and they are still being preserved in a location near the site of their origin,—and often by descendants of the very families to whom they originally belonged!